Confessions of a No Life

Buck Donic

Confessions of a No Life

A genuine and epic battle from an empty fridge to a six digits salary

First edition 2014
This impression 2014

www.buckdonic.com

ISBN: 978-0-578-13433-8

Notice to the Reader

While I do every effort to write properly, proof read and correct, please be aware that I am not a native English speaker. So any grammatical errors or unusual structures are not made out of carelessness.

A Desperate Try

How long a human being can survive without eating?

I never felt so embarrassed.

- Claudine! Come to see this!

The grocer was calling his wife to watch the show of me trying to sell him red syringe pens and laser watches.

I purchased them as a job lot from eBay then, wearing a suit and polished shoes, I was doing the doors in Grenoble; a small city in southeastern France.

- And which company did you say you work for?

- I am an independent distributor. I work for people who help businesses like yours to make load of money.

- Show me again

The wife was there; blank-faced; in her fifties; kitchen towel in her hand and a scarf with the same pattern over her head. Behind her a cuisine door was open filling the store with a smell of matured lard and onion soup. Patiently, I extracted another watch from its packaging and started my demonstration.

- This one has a red laser and can project up three different forms to the wall. Here you have the banana. There is also a Mickey Mouse and this funny smiling face. Obviously by night, it's more visible. We also do cell phone reception boosters and key chains with integrated lights.

Poker faces. No reaction whatsoever. My pitch was certainly successful but they were hiding their enthusiasm to get better price; clever.

- Did you sell a lot of "these things"?

- We are just starting in your city but in Paris, they sold them like crazy. Our goal is to help you making money. Our wholesale prices leave you with a very nice margin. Nobody has this item in your area. We import them directly from United States. People are fighting to get them over there.

My lovers weren't convinced by my presentation. The husband wiped out the leftover of a commercial grin from his face. I felt like he was going to ask me to leave. It was time for desperate measures! Reaching to my pocket, I produced a rectangular aluminum package.

- We also do fart bombs. These are the most powerful legally available for civilian use. You press here and it will give you about twenty seconds to vacate the place. I tried them at the university and I can testify that they are positively nauseating.

- Yeah, just leave now

Shame, they were not interested in buying fart bombs. I found myself on the street again. That day, I visited 5 or 6 convenience stores and newsagents with always the same result: "No, we are not interested".

I went back home defeated but not discouraged. Doing face to face cold sales of novelty items wasn't for me.

I had to try something else because my fridge was running out of food again.

* * *

Just months earlier, I almost died of starvation. It happened as I studied in one of the most prestigious Technology Institutes in Lausanne, Switzerland. I used electronic microscopes, super computers and complex equations to pierce the secrets of the atom, but I wasn't able to make enough money to buy 2000 calories a day necessary to sustain a living.

I remember when my card was declined at the till when I was shopping for food. The cashier asked me to try again while other customers behind me started showing signs of impatience. I knew that my account was empty but I hopped for some flexibility or a little overdraft; there were none. My only venue was to save the face:

- Well, I leave everything with you. I go to the bank to check what's wrong with this card and get some cash. Please keep these items for me.

- Sure. You'll find them with me or at the customer service desk when I am done with my shift

- No worries. Thank you again

I went home and lied in my bed for the next two weeks. I survived the first few days mixing sugar with water. Then my sugar ran out.

Searching frantically in old jackets, boxes and drawers, I found some change; just enough to buy the cheapest box of cat food. It was in a form of dry kibbles with "salmon and fish". In terms of taste, it wasn't Gordon Ramsay. Cats have a weird palate. You can trust me on this. However, in a survival situation, it made more sense to buy this food which was full of vitamins and proteins, rather than going for a salad.

Nobody could've helped me. Even my old aunt, my only relative in Switzerland, was at the hospital. Some charities used to distribute free meals in the center of Lausanne. But they were active during the winter only. It was summer time. Did you know that humans don't need to eat during the summer?

When you starve, the first 3 days are the most difficult. Once you pass that target, you don't feel the hunger anymore. Instead, you come to the realization that eating may not be as important as you always thought it is.

I was drinking plenty of water from the tap and sleeping most of the time. I was forcing myself to close my eyes and stop thinking. Even thinking uses calories and can drain the batteries faster.

"Don't move. Don't think. Close your eyes." That was my motto for the first ten days or so. I lost track of the time. An hour, a minute or a day were compressed to the same sensation of floating in the void. Without any effort, I was sliding in the darkness. I didn't have to force myself to stop thinking anymore. My brain was working slowly and was diving in long intervals of hibernation.

In these conditions, it took me days to come up with an obvious conclusion you – dear reader - draw already:

- I continue. I die.

Even through the fog of my idling intellect, I recalled a fridge; two big fridges in fact. They were located in a community center a mile from where I lived: second floor; no alarms; back door lock faulty. Mentally, I was preparing the raid. It was matter of life or death. I had just the energy to do that and it will be over. I realized that if I don't decide to take action that night, it would be too late. I would sleep longer and longer until I go forever. I was too dizzy to find anything wrong or terrifying about dying. It wasn't even painful; just a long and progressive slide to nowhere.

However, I voice deep inside told me that I had to move; now; at any cost. For some reason, I decided to follow it.

My watch was indicating 3 AM. Out the window, the night was perfectly dark. By some mysterious blessing, the conditions were ideal for an improvised burglary.

I wore a black pair of trousers and a black shirt. I also prepared a folded garbage bag for the loot. At least, if I were to steal from my neighbor, I had to do it sensibly and without attracting undue attention. This is even truer in Switzerland where police forces are very effective. Understandably, they don't appreciate it when civilians take wealth redistribution in their own hands.

At my surprise, the project gave me a new boost or energy but I was using my latest internal battery. Outside, the night was warm and quiet. I walked silently through a narrow path then a parking lot. I had to stop a couple of times as I felt too weak. Sometimes I heard noises that put me in alert but I had to continue my mission at any cost. After all, even being caught by the cops was a decent outcome. They have cells, doctors and food.

When I arrived at the crime scene, I discovered with relief that the lock was still in poor condition. I had just to push the door. Technically, it wasn't even a break-in. Using a gas lighter by short intervals, I managed to make my way to the kitchen at the second floor. I opened the door of the first fridge. There were a couple of salamis with a label in Russian, a bag of carrots, a massive piece of cheese, a box of eggs… in the freezer, I found two bags of chicken nuggets, a bag of French fries, a couple of pizzas, one box of vanilla ice cream. To be honest with you, I stole everything.

I didn't touch the wine or the alcohol. I was living through these rare and exceptional situations where a man is morally entitled to steal food only.

My bag was full and it wasn't in my best interests to extend the burglary beyond reasonable limits. Hauling the loot on my back, I carefully left the building I ransacked.

* * *

I remembered a story of a British explorer who was in a remote area of the African bushes but when it was time for lunch, he wore his 3-piece suit, dressed a table with glassware and cutlery then he sat to eat as a gentleman.

I pulled my table in the middle of the room and covered it with white napery. The set was completed with some mismatched cutlery then I sat to eat. I started with some fruits and cheese then I was overwhelmed and went to sleep.

In just two days, I recovered enough energy to walk to the nearest McDonald's restaurant and drop a basic resume. As they are always looking for staff, they hired me almost on the spot.

I spent three months in their kitchen. At the end, my feet were so swollen that I couldn't stand. When I looked to my shoes, they seemed so small that I couldn't believe that they were at my size one day.

When my alarm clock went off, I stopped it and continued sleeping. Later my manager rang. I told him to not to dial my number again. This page of my life was over.

But let me tell you something: if one day I have a kid, I want him to work a full season at McDonalds. In just 3 months, I learnt more there than in places where I spent much more considerable time.

In my street, there is a kebab shop. Five customers are queuing. The seller asks the first customer:

- What can I get you?

Predictably, the first customer would respond:

- I would like a kebab

- Sauce? Salad?

- Yes, please

Then the shop owner would take some bread and put it in an industrial toaster. After a minute, he will get it and go the grill to cut meat and put it in the bread. Then, he goes to fridge… It is a long, complex and serial process. When he is done, he goes then to next customer:

- What can I get you?

- I would like a kebab…

At this point in time, the last customer in the queue had already left. What they don't realize, is the fact that if it takes 6 minutes to make one kebab, it would take only 6 minutes and 30 seconds to make 5 kebabs.

Why some people sell hamburgers all their life and struggle to make ends meet while other sell similar hamburgers and open 3 restaurants a day? The difference is that McDonald's restaurants work at optimal efficiency. Things are done in parallel an in a well thought order to maximize production.

At the end of my adventure with McDonald's, I had a few hundreds Euros of saving and the firm motivation to work for myself online.

I didn't want to starve again; whatever the cost.

I declared a total war against misery.

I was going to be an internet warrior.

12

Part 1

Life as a Web Host

I would like to start this part by sharing with you the lessons I learnt in the field of the web hosting industry. Whatever the online business you are considering, you can be successful just by avoiding the mistakes I did as I had to learn everything the hardest way possible.

Like many things online, the web hosting industry is crowded and non-regulated. Anyone can open a web hosting service from his bedroom and claim anything. And believe me: many do!

I googled "web hosting" a couple of minutes ago and it showed more than 500 million results! There are literally thousands companies providing web hosting service. The market is not what it used to be, but guess what: as long as the internet exists, people will need web hosting companies.

Why I am saying that the market is not what it used to be? Mind you, in 2004 I had these sorts of customers:

- Someone who wants to creates a website to share his photos, the news of his family, get in touch with friends… Today, they don't need that. They go to **Facebook** and get this service for free.
- Someone who wants to publish videos taken in his church, his club or his own performances and interact with the audience. Does it ring a bell? Yes, now they go to **Youtube**, Vimeo or other video hosting platform.
- Someone who wants to share his resume/CV, uploads a couple of conservative photos and talk about his professional experience in order to get a job. I am sure it rings a bell also! Now, they all go to **LinkedIn**.

Imagine you run a shop where you make and sell bread for a living. Then arrive many companies that offer good bread for free in unlimited quantities. Overnight, you go from thousands breads sold daily to zero. You then decide to use the same tools to make pastries. You attract a new clientele but again: companies open stores and start giving away pastries in unlimited quantities.

That's how web hosting and web based services in general work. You always fight to create new ideas and elaborate revolutionary strategies in an ever changing environment. If you are looking for something easy and stable, this industry will kill you.

When I started in that field, I wrote down a couple of pages with generic assumptions and previsions. It was my "Business Plan". My thinking was simple:

- I sell a hosting service that people renew once a year.
- Year 2 down the line, I have already 2 streams of revenue: new customers, plus customers from previous year renewing their hosting.
- Year 3, I have 3 streams of revenue: new customers plus customers renewing from the previous couple of years…

You name it: an arithmetic progression with more and more money year after year.

Many people have projects and get quickly enthusiastic about them. They buy a domain name, they create a web site - or half of it - and then they forget about the whole story. It's very difficult to attract genuine and qualified traffic to a new website without investing big money in SEO and pay per click schemes. Without this, the website would just starve. A year later, many owners are not there when it's time to renew.

Some other people may leave your web hosting for any other reason. I will elaborate later about that.

If you add customers who leave you, to customers who are no longer interested in their project, you are losing between 30 to 50% of your customers every year. So you have to always chase for new customers to keep your earnings.

If you can't find new customers, your business is going to slow down and your revenue decline. The challenge is that the industry is always changing. The customer of 2014 will certainly have different expectations than the customer from the years before. You have always to be aware and adapt your offer to the market.

The day you can't adapt, you die.

* * *

I don't remember how the idea of a web hosting started in my mind. I don't want to make it up for the sake of this story but I know that my budget for the whole venture was 50 Euros. Ten years later and a lot of money after let me share with you something that – alone – would pay for the price of this book: don't trust any project that needs more than 50 Euros to start. What's the common point between HP, Amazon, Disney and Apple? They all started in a garage with a little or no budget.

Do you know why? If your idea is great and has a market it will make you money almost out of thin air. If your idea needs to start with a six digit budget, you are probably going to spend that budget until you hit the floor then close the business. I will tell you later about a friend of mine who had a "genius" idea: he sold his house for a six figure sum to start a business. He rented a building, hired people, purchased computers, hired an interior architect… and by the time he purchased the plants for his office more than half of the money was gone. Six month later, his account was deep in red and he had to close the business. You have to see big, but don't start big. Don't fake it! Don't try to be bigger than what you are in reality. Otherwise, you are not nourishing your business; you are nourishing your ego. Did you see the price tag of the latest Ferrari? It tells you that your ego is often too expensive for you.

Don't get me wrong. I said 50 Euros to start with but I would still follow you if your project needs 500, or 2000 Euros. The idea being: if you start with just a little money, you can't lose basically. There is only one road: success. And by the way: starting a business is like gambling. Whatever your idea, there is always a substantial risk of failure. Therefore, always spend the money you can afford to lose. Don't remortgage your house to start a business and don't use your retirement fund either! Bear with me a couple of lines here, I have something important to tell: often, the project you are launching is not the project of your life. This project may fail and give you valuable lessons for your next idea. And that next idea will bring you fortune. But what if you are broke after your first project? What if you are sleeping in the street already? Even if you learnt a lesson, you are no longer in position to apply it.

What I said in the previous paragraph may sound basic, but let me tell you something: we fail only for basic things. I never heard about a failure that was due to complicated circumstances. I would like also to share with you something from my exposure to the Jewish Kabbalah: in Hebrew, there are two different words for wisdom. One refers to wisdom as having knowledge and the other one refers to it as the ability to follow the knowledge we already have. How many things are obvious in your mind but not observable in your actions? Since Plato, many Westerners consider the knowledge as a virtue. Because of this, many people "know" but what's in their mind doesn't translate in any action. This book is not just about knowledge but about the use of that knowledge in actual situations.

I had 50 Euros and that was all. I was reluctant to use that money. I felt greedy. I went to ask my old aunt and she told me something I still remember: *"Look, with 50 Euros you are poor. With 0 Euros you are also poor. You have nothing to lose. Just go for it!"*

I went to eBay where I found someone selling reseller accounts. I took one without checking anything. He claimed that all resources were unlimited. So I thought I could sell without wondering about the limits. In the auction, the seller claimed more or less that he owned a data center.

What's good when you are new is that people don't know you. There are no reviews about you; no positive or negative. You are free to claim whatever you want in your sales pitch. I also claimed that I owned a data center and launched a website overnight.

To start my website, I installed a CMS and purchased a template at Template Monster (today I recommend ThemeForest.net). The time to create some plans and I began my promotion. Basically, I searched for all free classifieds websites (like Craigslist, Gumtree) and posted a nice text presenting the services I provide. I spent at least a couple of nights to this task. Sometimes I had to shorten my text because some websites have lower limits. I don't know how effective this was, but if you do it, I have one recommendation for you: go to Gmail and create an email address you give to this sort of websites. Expect tons of spam.

I also tried to promote on web forums, but I was too bold in my approach and got banned in a couple of posts. Administrators of these places make money by promoting their own sponsors and partners. They are really quick to eject people looking for a free ride.

I registered a new account to eBay and other auction websites then placed discounted packages for sale. Here, I would like to share with you another important key: don't always stick to eBay. Yes, eBay is the largest auction site but don't treat with disdain smaller competitors. I made more money in modest auction websites than on eBay. The main problem with eBay is the low average selling price. There are very wise shoppers looking for extreme bargains. Most of them won't buy anything if they don't feel that the seller is on massive loss. While on regional and niche auction websites, I found customers willing to pay more and I established a healthy relationship with them.

There are also local newspapers who can actually publish a classified advertisement for free or for a small fee. Later, you can try some national newspapers. Why I am talking newspapers for an online business? It seems awkward but let me share with you something: most people are not like you and me. Most people don't consult their email or Facebook page every 5 minutes if you see what I mean. Many potential customers have to create a website for their business or their activity but they are not really involved online. They don't go to forums. They still use Ask Jeeves as default search engine and they need help from their kids to start a Skype conversation. These customers have money to spend but are more present offline than online. They still take their breakfast and read newspapers. Here we raise another important point: don't think that everyone is like you. You are not creating a private club and are looking for likeminded individuals, okay? You need to go outside your comfort zone and search for people outside your usual circles.

Try to also target students in your area. They don't have a lot of money but they always have projects and if you price them well, they can send you a lot of customers. I used two different approaches with students. I went to the university and distributed flyers. If you are too shy for that, go to the university and find a display board. There are plenty of them where students put their extra-rooms to rent, or sell their books… etc. There you just publish something like: *"Job: looking for someone to distribute flyers. Contact me here:"* And provide an email address and a phone number. Also, while you are at the university place some leaflets on the display boards. When you talk to students, always be upfront about the discount you are offering.

Another clever tip I would like to share with you. Go to Fiverr.com and search under Advertisement section. You are going to find many people ready to distribute your flyers in their university in many countries. So without leaving your room, you can have people promoting your business in their university. What's good with this approach: again, you chase offline! Not all prospective customers, not even students, are online.

My First Customers

Do your promotion job as it is your main goal in life. Don't think about orders and money. They will come in their time. I got my first order after a couple of weeks. I can't tell you where the customer found me. It's difficult to say because most of them won't tell you. They are just here to buy your service. However, what you can do is to add the question to your contact or order form. It will help you a lot to see which marketing vector is the most efficient for your business.

Here, I want also to stop and share with you a critical business advice. Look what people usually do: they sell a variety of products. Then, when they review their figures, they see that some products are not selling as well as they wanted. So most people do the following: they invest more marketing on these struggling products! This is a big mistake. Invest more on the product that sells! So for marketing, it's the same story: if you see that most people are coming from university advertisement, it means you are on the good wave with that. Surf it! Put even more advertisement at the university and be even more present. In other words, invest on success not on failure.

To attract customers, I offered a free month trial. A free trial is more powerful than a 100% money back guarantee. Because the customer feels that he is taking zero risks. It is better for him to test and leave if he doesn't like your service than to pay and chase you for a refund. From your perspective, you are losing nothing. You create an account on an existing platform and send a welcome email. It takes you 10 minutes but this is an investment. When the customer tries your service, he needs to change his DNS, upload his data... basically doing very boring things. Once his website is online on your servers, a month goes by quickly and the customer is hooked. If you provided him with a good service during that month, he is going to stay with you.

I tell you also why this free trial method is so powerful. Let's face it: there are some bad customers outside. You don't want them at any cost. There are the people who are always unsatisfied and very vocal about it. They will snap at every incident (bounced email, server crash, lost password...). They have time in hand and can post very nasty reviews about you. Just a few of these customers can literally ruin your business and your brand **forever**. We don't care if these reviews are deserved or not. People will read them and take them in account. I will explain later how to deal with these bad reviews. But to return to our topic, with the free trial you have only satisfied customers who signed up with you. All others would leave and this is a very good thing for you.

If you don't want to deal with a free trial, that's fair enough, but you have to create another no-damage exit strategy. For example, offer a serious 100% refund policy. Because whatever happens, if people take their money back, they feel less entitled to criticize you. Most of the time, they are just happy for the free ride and go somewhere else. It's only when they can't get their money that they feel entitled to damage your reputation in return. Their rational is: *I lost $100 I will post negative reviews and make them lose $1000 to teach them a lesson.* You don't want this lesson because it can cause unlimited damage to web-based business.

Reputation & Bad Reviews

Many people have the habit of posting reviews online. However, look at this equation:

- Most happy customers never post a review
- Most frustrated customer always post a review

Let add some other items:

- Most people search for reviews before ordering
- Relatively few negative reviews can kill your brand

If your brand is killed, it means that you are going to see no order in the foreseeable future. Relatively few unhappy customers can ruin your business. Some of them can be malicious. They troll and post multiple negative reviews on all websites they can find. One single troll can kill your house and have you shut down your doors. Take this very seriously.

Here are some approaches you can follow very carefully since day one to start building a positive online reputation:

1 – On regular basis, write emails to your customers asking them to post their opinion about you and send you the link to receive a reward. As incentive you can give them more data storage or 20% off their next bill. Don't solicit every customer. Select customers who have had recent good experience with your support and who sent to you some positive feedback already.

2 – Create a moderated board or a subpage on your website to share positive reviews you receive by email. Request customer permission and remove any private information before sharing.

3 – Ask your close friends and family to post positive reviews about you. Don't write the reviews yourself, just tell them what to say and let them word it. If the person is not too technical, ask her to show you the review before posting. To sound believable, it needs to be balanced from neutral to positive. If you want to put something negative in a positive text, make sure it's not against you. Like: *yeah, I had just one incident with them where they suspended my accounts for nonpayment while I was on holiday and unable to read my email for a couple of weeks. However, on my return the situation was quickly fixed by their support department.* You see here even if the customer shares an incident, every reader would understand that the whole thing is from customer fault.

May be you don't like to cheat and get your family to post reviews for you. But let me tell you something: they all do it. Even big corporations send internal emails to their employees asking them to vote for a product or post positive reviews. Many people, organizations or companies sneakily edit their Wikipedia page.

It's a silly world let me break it to you. But it gets even worse when you leave your business in a situation where a miscreant teenager can close it down. Your defense is to have an overwhelming majority of positive reviews to balance any negative review that may – God forbid – happen in the future.

When posting fake reviews, be careful to stay under the radar. Ideally, on any website post a fake review every 4 or 5 genuine reviews. Otherwise, post one review every 6 to 8 weeks. If you travel, profit from your hotel connection to post reviews as they will come from different geo-locations. Don't use proxies to achieve the same result! Many proxy addresses are well known and some of them even forward your actual IP address. Don't play with proxies; it can just backfire because the IP is not the only way to identify a device online. I will detail this in another book, but for now, keep in mind that if you want to publish some fake reviews, do it from different locations with different devices or computers.

Still, what if someone posts a negative review? Don't leave a negative review without answering. Check on Tripadvisor for example. All serious hotels and restaurants read their reviews and post their comments to any published issue. As an exercise, go to Tripadvisor, chose any decent hotel chain like Ritz and read the reviews and how their respond to them. Use the same approach to manage your reputation online. Respond honestly to any legitimate concern and explain what you did to avoid it in the future.

There is also an important point I would like to demonstrate. Read these two reviews and think about them:

Review one:

I hosted my website for almost a year with this host. The first six months, it worked just fine and I had nothing to complain about. I just logged one ticket one day because I was unable to create a new ftp account and this was fixed promptly. Later issues started. The server crashed twice in a single month. My uptime went down to 95% and I had myself to deal with many complaints from my own customers. As I am web designer, I also have the responsibility to host my own customers' sites and data. To avoid further incidents, I decided to leave this host.

Review two:

This company is run by a bunch of scammers and retards. They stole my money. I hosted my website with them but I never got any service. Their servers are always down. Don't go with them! If you sign-up with them, your website will be always down and they will take your money and run away. Avoid! Avoid! Avoid!

The first review is a genuine opinion. The best way to deal with it is to provide a courteous and prompt response. Something like this would do:

> *Hello,*
>
> *We are sorry to hear that we have let you down on this occasion. Last year we had indeed a server that crashed twice in a short period of time. When the first crash occurred, we summoned an onsite Engineer from Dell who replaced the memory and signed off the machine for return to production. Sadly the server crashed again a couple of weeks later. At that point, it was obvious that something was wrong with the motherboard. To not to take any risk, we decided to replace the whole server. The replacement box has been running continuously for 198 days as I am posting. Again, we are*

sorry that this issue affected your confidence on our web hosting services. Please don't hesitate to contact me to <email address> if you have any questions.

Thank you.

Here, you address the main concern. Explain that the central issue raised in the review was fixed and give your contact details as a way to bring the conversation **offline**. The customer may or may not contact you. But from the perspective of anyone reading the review, you are honest and open to discussion. In many countries (such as France) responding to a review is a right. Under many jurisdictions, it is illegal for a website or an offline publication to deny you the right to respond to a review about your business. Check your local laws.

The second review is of a different nature. It's libelous. I would like to invite you to spend a couple of hours on google searching for the difference between opinion/review and libel. While the law protects opinions as free speech, no one can hide behind that to insult you, threaten you or make false statements of facts. The second review is full of insults and wrong facts. The reviewer can't say that your servers are down all the time because it's not true. He may not tell other to avoid you. He can't say that you are a thief or scammer if you haven't been convicted by a Court of Law. Even if you actually ran away with his money, you are not a scammer until convicted. Writing publicly that you are "a thief" is defamation or a libel. You can sue the reviewer for that and also the website hosting such a review.

Indeed, you are not going to sue anyone for now. You are managing a small business and have no money and no time to sue people. However, as the review is illegal in its nature, you have an edge to get it removed. Most people when unhappy tend to include libelous items in their reviews. You can leverage on that on get rid of the review in question. Here is an example of an email you can send to the webmaster of the website publishing the review:

Hello,

During our visit to your website, this page attracted our attention: <URL>

The review posted there by an anonymous user doesn't represent a fair opinion but a libel punished by law. We are a well-established business trading legally and with good reputation and standing in the community.

While we are delighted to interact with our customers when they post online comments, we always take very seriously any false statement published to harm our reputation. The review also contains abuse and insults towards our company and our staff.

21

*As this material is illegal in nature and represents a **liability** for your website, we kindly ask you to remove it.*

Again, as a Web Services company we value freedom of speech and always appreciate when our customers post genuine reviews. We thrive on positive reviews and we learn from negative ones. But insults and defamation are not things we can tolerate.

Thank you for your collaboration and our best wishes to your website.

<Signature>

I don't know any sensible webmaster who wouldn't remove the review after receiving this email. I got some defamatory posts removed within hours with this approach. No one wants to get to court to stand for a stupid story posted by a troll. If the website owner ignores you or refuses to remove the offending content, go to this host. For this, do the following:

- Ping the domain name of the website: it will give you his IP address
- Do a whois on the IP address: it will give away his host and the abuse report address

Email, or if you wish, send a registered mail with the following:

Dear <Host> Staff,

A website (<URL>) is using your network to publish defamatory and libelous content about our business. This material contains abuse, insults, threats and false statements that harm our reputation as a well-established and legally trading Company. We claim that this content is harming our reputation, causing distress and financial loss.

Before taking any legal proceeding, we assumed that the owner of the aforementioned website is in good faith and we tried to contact him to find a solution. As he is not responding, we are contacting you as his Service Provider to assist us in removing this illegal content.

Here is a copy of the offending message: <copy of the review>

We appreciate your assistance in this.

Best Regards

<Signature>

Service providers and data centers are very aggressive with abuse. If you involve them, they can use their authority and get the webmaster to remove the offending content. I have already seen servers down for similar issues. Typically, they give the webmaster or his host 24 hours to respond before they block the server.

If you know who is posting this material, don't send him an email, go directly to a lawyer and send him a *"Cease and Desist Letter"*. In the letter your lawyer will ask him to cease his harassment activity and remind him the law. He will also ask him to go online wherever he posted defamatory content and remove it to avoid further legal proceedings. If this person is in a different country, search online for a lawyer in the same country and ask him to write and send this letter for you. Your troll would feel the heat even stronger if your lawyer is close to him.

Other important places where people post reviews are web forums. I ask you to not to go there! If these reviews are within legal limits, ignore them. If not, use the same proceeding above and start by sending an email to the host and the webmaster. But don't go there to post. In forums people are a community and any poster has a number of virtual friends ready to help in any situation. So if you respond, they will all come to post and you will find yourself one against many. The thread will attract more audience, stay on the top longer and attract even more search engines. The only exception I make is for professional forums where you can go and respond only once. Post only one single response and show clearly that you would like to bring the conversation offline as you are bound by your privacy agreement that prohibits you from discussing customer issues publicly (Even if the customer himself brings a matter to the public, you are still bound by your privacy agreement and cannot yourself disclose the same information). As always, your message must be concise, clear and professional. Show respect for the customer and the audience. Make it clear that you understand his concerns and what you are doing, or what you did, to address them. If there are any factual inaccuracies, you can also correct them without any aggressively towards the customer. End your post by giving your contact details or a link to your contact page and stop the conversation there. It's not in your interest that the conversation goes beyond that point.

I know that I am taking some of your time in this topic but believe me, your online reputation is your best asset. If this reputation is damaged, you are gone.

Action Needed: Now, I invite you to think a minute about your brand and online reputation. How bad is the situation? Use various search engines and make a serious audit about your online reputation. If you have more negative than positive reviews, it means that you have bad reputation and your brand in not suitable for business anymore. Try to learn from your mistakes and start thinking about a new name for your business. The sooner you do it, the sooner you will start earning money again.

* * *

At the peak of my web hosting business, I used to spend up to 1000 Euros a month on Google Adwords. I used to get 5000 Euros of business out of every 1000 Euros spent. It's very important to be honest and specific in your advertisement. If you sell your hosting for 50 Euros, don't advertise it as free hosting. Because your goal is not that the whole humanity clicks (remember: you pay per click) but only "qualified" individuals. A qualified customer is someone who is very likely to purchase.

Google Adwords return on investment declined very quickly for me. In my last campaign ever, I spent 800 Euros in 2 weeks for zero return! I started searching and I found out that some people have setup *clicking farms* in India and Pakistan. Just Google this: *"click for rupees"* or *"Get paid for clicking"*. Basically the scammers create websites with a lot of valuable keywords then they install Google AdSense there. This will display advertisements from announcers like me. Then, the guys in the clicking farm use different IPs to click frantically on the advertisements. The budget is gone without any return.

Some places also use tricks to generate clicks. I found forums where to download a pirated game or a DVD people have to click on Google advertisements to reveal the actual download links purposefully hidden by a JavaScript. Other webmasters have the habit to click every day on the advertisements displayed on their own websites. They do it once from home, once from school, once from their work, once from a friend Wi-Fi… etc.

This is indeed illegal and Google does its best to chase this fraudulent activity but from the perspective of an announcer, you spend the money and you see no result at all.

In any case, if you want to go with Google Adwords make sure your ads are not displayed anywhere else but in the Google search engine **itself**. Avoid what they call the "Display Network" as this refers to millions of websites over which Google has no control. I even heard about some people clicking on their competitors' ads just to smoke their budget!

Don't get me wrong. Google Adwords is a powerful network that can bring you quality leads and serious business. But my point is: using Google Adwords is **rocket science**. If you don't want to lose your money, you have to dedicate time and efforts to master the subject. Buy at least a couple of highly rated and recent books on Amazon and read them while taking notes.

When you feel ready to start your campaign, go to eBay and search for "Adwords voucher". You will always find nice vouchers with up to 90% discount. A $100 voucher typically sells for $10. You can create a new Adwords account and fund it with a voucher to finance your first trials and errors. Note than more often than not, you will have to put some real money (usually $25) before you can redeem the voucher.

But again, treat it seriously and go there only when you really understand all its aspects.

Horror Story: Unreliable Partner

When I started my business, I got in touch with a young guy who started more or less in the same time. While he was a sole trader, he managed to give his website an impressive corporate look. He showed photos of his "headquarters", "offices" and posted a lot of customers and "employees" testimonials.

One day, he told me that he rented a couple of racks in a data center and he was wondering if I wanted to join him and share the space. That perspective was interesting for me. To share the cost of the place and having my own servers sounded like a great idea. I asked him to give me some time to think about the whole story and do some math to see if it is something financially viable for me. To be honest with you, it was financially interesting but something, like a sixth sense, kept me from jumping in it immediately.

A month later, I heard the news: his company closed down leaving thousands of people offline without access to their data. Various web forums were filled with angry or desperate customers trying to get answers from somebody. Occasionally there were one-liner posts giving some hope: *apparently, they had a massive denial of service attack and they are trying to bring the servers up again.* Or: *they have a big problem with a Cisco router and everything will be back again in the evening...*

Nothing came back again and many people lost their websites and often months, if not years, of hard work.

What happened? Many months later I got in touch with the person responsible of all this mess. He closed all his online accounts and was avoiding the internet all together. When I asked him what happened, I wasn't expecting the answer:

- *yeah, well. I went with my family to ski. I met there with some friends and decided to stay longer with them. I forgot totally that I had to pay the racks. When I came back home, I found out that everything was down for a few days already. As I was tired of doing web hosting, I decided to forget about the whole story and let this business die.*

The problem with these people is that they give sole traders a bad name. Customers would never trust a hosting company if they can't check its credentials and make sure they are dealing with a genuine big corporate.

In fact, my own grand-father died saying: "don't take any associates". I prefer to have partners or employees but otherwise, I work alone. I don't want my success to depend on anyone.

Horror Story: Free hosting

Some people think about giving away free service in the hope that their customers would one day upgrade to paid contracts. This is not true. It never worked and it will never work. People who add the word *free* to their google searches are not a qualified audience. They don't want to pay for a service because they don't have budget for that, or they think the service is not important for them or maybe they don't even have a credit card to pay online. Whatever their reasons, they are certainly respectable folks but they are not interesting to do business with. Also if you offer a free hosting, you are going to attract a lot of unwanted audience: spammers, scammers... etc. If they don't pay, you cannot verify their identity.

I remember one day a guy contacted me asking to rent a server ready for web hosting. I had a spare machine at the time and I sealed a deal with him. He paid promptly the first 2 or 3 months then suddenly stopped responding to my payment reminders. I chased him for more than a week then I decided to shut down the machine. Many people when they leave, they don't bother to inform you. They just stop paying.

A couple of days later, I started receiving emails from heated crowd asking me to bring the server online again. They contacted the data center and were given my contact details as the owner of the network. In response to these complaints, I decided to start the box and login to the control panel to estimate the damage. They were like 300 websites! And believe it or not, most of them were professional ones: small and mid-size businesses, some organizations, a few blogs, forums and a lot of ecommerce portals. I couldn't understand how these people placed their websites in a new free hosting service managed by a teenager. I helped a couple of guys to collect their backups but – mind you – their weren't ready to pay for a proper hosting, they wanted just to take their data and try to find another free host.

I didn't want to put myself in a middle of a mess created by an irresponsible guy and his even more irresponsible customers. Some of them were sending rude and threatening emails asking for free service or their files. I went ahead and formatted the server because someone else accepted a quote for it. After all, if they weren't ready to pay, their data is probably not important for them.

Horror Story: too good to be true

Mid-2000s, a dedicated server with 2 Gb of RAM was considered as a serious machine. Mainstream servers were dispatched with 512 Mb to 1 Gb of RAM in most cases. I remember when a US company inundated web hosting forums with crazy prices for servers with 16 Gb or RAM! They were renting them for $200/month with massive other specs and associated services. I was one of the happy first customers to secure mine. They sent me the credentials within hours and I logged in to the box. Everything was as described. So far so good!

The project was to move my biggest accounts there. I had some very busy forums generating a lot of MySQL database requests. These were the best candidates for that migration. However, before to proceed, I needed to talk with the webmasters to find a suitable maintenance window when the transfer can be actually done. They needed a few days to inform their users and make their arrangements for the operation. It took me some time going back and forth between all participants but they were all thrilled to get more power for the same price.

Ten days later, I was still negotiating with my customers to schedule a night or a weekend to start moving their data. The server was ready to accept them with Apache, MySQL, PHP… and all other software installed and configured.

Literally hours before the big transfer, the server stopped responding. I thought it crashed and I sent an email to the provider asking for a reboot. A few hours later, without any response, I went to the web forum where I initially found this company. Basically there were plenty of nervous people asking for updates as their machines weren't online.

The whole thing sounded really fishy to me. I informed my customers that I am cancelling the transfer until further notice and I went chasing for news. The provider wasn't returning calls or emails.

It took me a week to get the full picture. In fact, an American IT Company had hundreds of powerful servers in racks when it went bankrupt. As the data center was paid in advance, the company was given a notice of a month before the whole infrastructure is disconnected. A couple of employees decided to rent the servers in the meantime and pocket the money.

These scammers were well aware about the situation and knew that the contract with the data center was being terminated. They priced them at a fraction of their market value to rent them quickly and profit from the opportunity window. During a short time frame many people uploaded their files to these machines and lost it when they were disconnected for good.

I never recovered my money but my damage was limited as I never put any data in my server.

The lesson here is to be careful with crazy opportunities especially when they are new in the market. Always take your time and analyze everything from a distance.

Horror Story: overselling in Germany

I hosted a customer with a very busy portal. His website had a forum, an active video section and a lot of articles with a large audience.

Initially he was on a shared account but his developers wanted more flexibility and a root account access. The only way forward was to provide them with a dedicated server. I found a German provider with which I worked a couple of times in the past. On a web forum, they were promoting *"unmetered"* dedicated servers on a 100 Mbps line.

As my customer was pulling between 2 and 3 Mbps with spikes to 10 Mbps, I felt that the offer was good for him and even allows some room for progression. I rented the server and prepared it with all the software needed to host the website. A day later my customer started uploading his data in the machine and the production started.

A couple of weeks down the line all of a sudden the port was capped to 256 Kbps without any notification. From the perspective of my customer, everything went down. The videos were not playing and many attempts were necessary just to display the header of his main page.

I logged a ticket with my provider but they ignored it. In the meantime I was receiving angry calls and emails from my customer and his team of developers. It was very hard for me to justify what was going on.

I went to another provider and rented a server. I spent a sleepless night preparing it then sent the credentials of the new machine to my customer with my apologies. However, it didn't totally fix the issue as the customer wanted to pull his data from the original server. But as the connection was capped, transferring files was painfully slow. Again I logged a support ticket asking the German provider to open the port just for a few hours for us to pick-up our files. They closed the ticket without responding.

Subsequently I lost that customer. It was a costly experience because he could have been a referral to a large community if everything worked out as expected.

Months later, I analyzed the market and realized that the price of bandwidth is ridiculously high in German data centers. This is probably due to some limitations in their network infrastructure comparatively to other countries. For some complicated political and economic reasons, this country didn't invest enough to bring its internet to European standards. As result, anyone who claims renting a server on an unmetered 100 Mbps is plainly lying. My guess is that they run a few hundreds servers on a single 100 Mbps line then they do pruning to cap or block the top users.

Again, it was my fault here to not to investigate thoroughly before going for this offer. Whatever your business field is, you are never the Alpha and the Omega. You always rely on other Business to Business (B2B) providers to build your product. Your final service to the customer is a good as your choice of B2B suppliers.

Investigate local laws, practices and policies before you shop for any product or service for your own business.

Horror Story: Servers in Florida

Besides local laws and practices, you need also to check the weather of the countries you order services or products from. If the consistence and the continuity are essential factors, it might be advisable to avoid that are subjects to floods and hurricanes.

When I found a cheap supplier in Florida, I didn't think twice before renting a couple of servers. The machines were intended to host some low-cost accounts. Some of my customers wanted to be online at the lowest rate possible regardless of any other consideration.

These machines performed very well and within a couple of months they were full of happy webmasters. Even if they weren't paying a lot, they didn't require any support. Basically, it was easy money.

One day, both machines went down at the same minute. I wasn't alarmed as it was obvious that the data center was experiencing some temporary outage. I just posted an acknowledgment in my support forum then went to bed.

Next morning, at my horror, the machines were still offline. Even the supplier website was out of reach. I checked my bill. The boxes were paid in time. There was no reason from them to disconnect my service. I logged a case and started emailing my customer to buy some time. Usual crisis communication *"Yes, we know"*, *"we are doing the maximum right now"*, *"our engineers have been already engaged in this"*, *"we will offer a free month hosting"*...

Later that day, I received the bad news. A hurricane with a Spanish sounding name hit the area and the whole data center was down. A couple of days later, my machines were still in the dark. The pressure from my customers was too high. In the web hosting business, even an hour outage is already difficult to justify. Two days, it's the time you need to go out of business.

I had to call the supplier many times to get someone on the line. It was a young support engineer. After a short conversation, I felt that he was an honest and straight talking buy. I asked him to provide an ETA for the restoration of my boxes. The answer was very clear:

- Never. The machines are deep below six feet of water.

Shortly after this incident, the supplier filed for bankruptcy. In my turn, I lost that entry level part of my business. My customer never recovered their data and most of them didn't maintain an offsite backup.

Horror Story: Investing on the Wrong people

One year after I started my company, I was contacted by a guy from Africa. He sent an email explaining that he was motivated to create a hosting business and seek customers in his country but he had no money to start with.

I called him and we had a conversation. I felt like he was really passionate about technology and available to launch a web hosting project.

Myself, I felt a business opportunity for both of us. Actually in Africa there are many fast growing markets where more and more major corporations go. You may sell your products or services for a lower price, but you can sell a much higher volume. However, I can't go to Africa alone. Having an associate in place to deal with locals is a must. In other hand, with no capital and a little knowledge, this guy needed me to realize his project. It was an obvious win-win situation for both of us.

I registered a good domain name for him and prepared a server for the hosting. I purchased a template at Templates Monster and spent a few days populating it with presentations, plans, FAQ... etc.

This was my first mistake already. I should have asked him to create a decent website himself and then show me the result for approval. If you start a joint venture and you do 100% of the job, what's the point of being associated with someone? Does he just sit and share the revenue? How can you measure your partner's motivation and how effective is he if you do everything yourself?

I then walked him through the process of creating accounts and provision various services. I also explained how to support his end users and avoid most issues. To conclude, I left the door open for him to escalate to me any problem he can't tackle locally.

To encourage him even further to go to the market, I told him to keep 100% of the revenue he makes the first year.

Let me stop here for a moment: this was a major **mistake**. If you want to do a joint venture with someone, you **must** enforce good practices from day one. If you make even 1 dollar and I am with you at 30%, you give me 30 cents. If it doesn't happen from the beginning, it will never happen.

Well, he started promoting the business and creating accounts in the server.

I spent long hours coaching him, giving advice and also updating software and doing Linux administration tasks.

A year later, I contacted him to start talking money. Basically, I didn't ask for money the first year because I was looking big. I wished for the project to succeed in a country where no webhost was actually present. Being the first there, I wanted to attract big accounts like corporate customers and governmental administrations. Well, my partner complained that the market wasn't good; that he lost customers the other day because the server crashed... etc.

I decided to hear his arguments and give him more time. My goal wasn't to create rush or sense of pressure but to drive the business to success.

To make a long story short, three years later he was still hosted in my infrastructure without giving back a single buck. As I was cleaning and restructuring my financial affairs, I contacted him and made it clear that I was no longer in position to support alone this partnership. I gave him some time to think about it and get back to me with a clear roadmap for our venture. As he felt that I was serious, he spent the next few days sneakily moving out his customers to a server he rented from a US provider.

A few months later, he even had the guts to fire an email to ask me to transfer the domain name to his ownership! That domain name was my legal property. I chose it. I registered it and I renewed it year after year using my personal funds.

I know no one who wouldn't have forwarded that domain traffic to a porn website. But it's not "me" to do that. I am a man of honor. My actions depend on my own values and my own judgment only. They are not submitted to other parties' actions. I am not in this world to lose and make people lose. Either I win or I quit with elegance. Believe it or not, I released the domain name and he is using it to this day.

The lesson here is to set clear goals to any partnership and enforce agreed rules since day one. If you have no time for a partnership, you are too busy for that, have other priorities… or just it's not working as your hoped for then just get out! Don't stay there forever. If something didn't work during the last 12 months, chances are slim that it would work better during the next 12 months. Get over it. Take your cards from the deal with minimal losses for you and focus on winning ideas. If you stay on dodgy deals, you are going just to accumulate loss and grief.

Doing dedicated: between profit and Ponzi scheme

When my shared web hosting reached its cruising altitude, I decided to introduce dedicated servers to my offers. I had two reasons to decide that at the time. Some resellers were outgrowing their accounts and I didn't want them to leave for another provider who could provision a dedicated server. The other point is that I wanted my company to look bigger by offering all sort of services we find with major suppliers.

My initial approach was to rent servers from various places, add some services (like local support, management and monitoring) then sublet them to my customers with a markup. On my website, I published a list of offers for servers I didn't have actually. But I had accounts with the suppliers and was familiar with their products and provisioning process.

I sublet one server, then two, then three… my apparent margin wasn't great: 10 to 20% per machine. For example, I pay myself $100/month for a box and my customer pays me $110 for it. In fact, when we subtract Paypal and conversion fees – if any – my benefit was between $5 and $7 per month per server.

Any time in your business you see such an unfavorable ratio between the money invested (here $100) and the benefit (here $5), it means you are taking a huge financial risk. If you look at this from another angle, you will see that I was risking $100 to make only $5. It means that for any unsuccessful transaction where I lose $100, I needed 20 successful transactions (1 year and 8 months) just to break even!

With that sort of schemes, you have often short term small benefits then long term big loses that wipe out everything you have earned so far.

In my case, the pattern was the following. A customer asks for a server. I go to my provider to rent a machine, prepare it and turn it back to the end user. Assume this is a $100 machine I sublet for $110. So after 6 months, my benefit is around $30 when you deduct all the expenses. A customer who stays 6 months is a good customer! In that volatile market, only a minority of them would stick around for that long. More often than not, 3 to 4 months is the average time they keep the machine.

So here I am with a $30 short term benefit.

Then, month 7 down the line I contact the customer for payment and he asks for a short delay because he is travelling. Well, what do you do here? You close the server and end-up treated like a monster in web forums? *Okay, well, thank you Mr. Customer, I allow you that time.* Then my provider sends his bill: $100. I can't ask for a delay myself because I am trading with big corporations and everything is automated. I can't even talk to a human being. It's either I pay online or my server would be formatted and *returned to the pool.* So I pay $100 hoping that my customer won't let me down.

A week later, no news from the customer: my only option is to shut down the server and calculate my loss so far -$70. If I am lucky, I would find a customer within 2 weeks. During that time, I was the happy owner of the server. The cost of that ownership is $50. I need 10 months of punctual payments just to recover that.

I didn't really saw this pattern until I had more than 20 servers up and running. Every new customer was in fact providing short term benefits for me to use to compensate long term losses from other customers.

To make the situation even worse, I rented some servers on a 1 year contract to get better prices myself. But I couldn't enforce such a long term commitments with my own customers. Consequently for just a few bucks a month, I was shifting the contract responsibility from the client and bearing it myself.

From my immediate perspective, I watched the money coming but I was always at loss. I could invoice and receive 2000 Euros on week one, then I would pay 2200

Euros to my providers on week two. If I were lucky, I would pay just 1950 Euros to my suppliers and keep 50 Euros for the hassle. But again more often than not, I was at loss. In fact other parts for my business were compensating.

When I realized the amount of money I was wiring to providers in various countries, I decided to go higher in the food chain and rent my own racks. Be my own provider and stop paying monthly fees for servers, extra-disks and extra-memory.

Going Dedicated: Colocation

I compared the offers from some data centers and rented a couple of racks with 10 Mbps of transfer on each on a 100 Mbps symmetric line. Any extra Mbps of data transfer would have been charged for 35 Euros. Welcome in a world with no overselling: you use it, you pay it! Yourself, you can sell your 10 Mbps to 50 customers if you like, but you pay what they actually use whatever the price is.

I established my shopping list. Here is what I needed:

- Servers: 1U form factor is the best because they don't take that much of space
- Network switches: because there is 1 single network cable per rack. Hence it is meant to be connected to a switch then the servers are connected to the remaining ports of that switch
- Power switches: to be able to recycle the power remotely on any server to reboot it when everything else fails
- Cables: the easiest bit
- Rack hardware: screws and rails are not provided

I asked Dell and HP to provide a quote for servers with onsite support. They quoted me like 3000 Euros per unit! By pushing to the maximum, I could have rented these machines for 150 Euros/month each. It means that I needed 20 months of continuous operations just to get the price of the server back. But in fact, my high-end server today would look less shining in just 12 months. Every few weeks, there are faster CPUs, bigger hard drives, better memory modules... My 3000-Euro box would be outdated in just a few moons. I might be able to rent it for 150 Euros the first year, but I would have to compromise around 100 Euros on year 2 and 50 Euros on year 3 if the machine is still alive. That's 3600 Euros in 3 years.

I am not done yet: I need to include the part of that server in the price of the rack, the bandwidth and the power. Well, we are looking to 300 Euros per year. So, after 3 years, I would have charged 3600 Euros to my customer (assuming the machine is rented 100% of the time) and paid 900 Euros towards the hosting fees for the machine. So I have 2500 Euros in hand. I am still 500 Euros short! I can sell it on eBay then and try to recover some of my loss.

After doing some math, it was clear that HP and Dell offers were out of my reach and unsuitable for my business model anyway. I am not even talking about the Cisco switch at 2000 Euros and the power switch from APC for a similar price.

My only viable option was to go to eBay try my luck. I decided to choose my components, buy a chassis and build my custom machines. I had to find motherboards, CPUs, disks… and some parts difficult to find: like extra-flat 1U heat-sinks and fans. Special 1U power supplies were not very common in Europe and I had to buy them from United States. When you include shipping fees, Customs tax for parts coming from abroad I was well above my expected budget when I started building my machines.

It was laborious to fit parts from different origins inside a chassis thick just like a couple of Mars bars. I spent countless hours trying to find the most effective routing for the cables to maximize the airflow. For a few servers, it was necessary to use balsa wood and superglue to attach elements. Some motherboards were fitted with a block of sound connectors. They were bulky enough to prevent me from closing the server lid. Who needs to ever plug earphones or speakers to a server? I went for the only option possible: I saw them off!

My appliances were all different depending on the origin of the parts. Some were messy and looked dodgy some other were clean and neat.

Always on eBay, I found an old Cisco Catalyst 2900 switch with 24 ports. There were zillions of them going for 30 Euros when not too rotten. They are capable of auto-negotiation at 10 or 100 Mbps. They also have a management page where it's possible to create virtual networks, bind ports and perform other basic functions. However, as these switches were too old - probably from Windows 3.11 era – the management page wasn't compatible with any up to date web browser. I had to go to Oldversion.com to download a prehistoric release of Netscape that worked with that.

As APC power switches were too expensive, I searched for other brands. In the US version of eBay there were secondhand Baytech RPC-3 selling for $50. I used Auctionsniper.com to place a bid during the last 5 seconds to bargain some of these switches. They looked robust and were intuitive to configure. Every switch had 8 power plugs that could be assigned to different accounts allowing the customer to log-in and reset his own plug if the server freezes.

I spotted a good tariff with FedEx Ground Services then I shipped all my hardware in a palette to the data center. To spare some money, I kept 3 servers to take with me by train. I couldn't afford a car at the time or even a driving license.

The big day came in and I took the train to the data center where my FedEx palette was waiting for me. It was a 10 hour journey to Amsterdam with a few connections. Go by plane did you say? It wasn't possible because I had to take a backpack full of tools and a caddie with 3 servers weighting 15kg/33lbs each.

When I left the last train at Amsterdam Schiphol airport, I was tired and hungry but still excited about getting into a data center for the first time in my life. I walked outside and crossed the street to the taxis station. I approached the first car. The driver stared at me with disgust. I didn't look like the typical tourist just landing from New York and ready to drop 150 Euros to be driven to his hotel. Nervously, I showed a piece of paper with the address of the data center printed on it. For a few seconds he looked at it trying to measure the distance then he said:

- No, I don't take you there. Too close. Only 8 kilometers [5 miles]

I approached the second vehicle, but the driver hid behind the rules of his corporation:

- I can't take a customer unless I am at the first position in the waiting line

No point to try to negotiate with them. They wanted their American tourist or nothing. I approached a bus driver and explained the situation. He was kind enough to unfold a map and locate my address there. There was a bus line with a stop almost one mile from the data center. It wasn't brilliant but I had no better solution in hand…

The bus dropped me in a middle of an industrial zone with planes flying by at low altitude to land on Schiphol runways. On any direction, there were only big warehouses secured by gates, barbed wire and surveillance cameras. From time to time a van or a semi drove by but there were no pedestrians to be seen. Go and find a data center!

I don't know how many miles I actually walked pulling my heavy trolley. From the planes passing over, I must have looked like a Roman carriage with a human replacing the horse. I found a data center and rang the bell. A security guard approached. He looked me as if I was a battered dog. I showed him my access references and he walked with me to a lobby. A young lad entered the numbers in a computer then opened a large register to search inside for a while. He asked me to hold then he picked-up his phone and called his manager for assistance. Something was going wrong.

The manager came in and entered my name and access code in the computer then shook his head and turned to me:

- Sir, you are in the wrong data center.

I found just the strength to utter something like: *"are you sure?"*

- Absolutely.

I was a few miles from my destination. Showing some compassion, the manager brought a set of keys and asked me to follow him to the parking lot. A few minutes later, he dropped me in front of the correct address. Eventually, I made it!

I spent the whole night installing my servers. The data center was noisy and surprisingly warm. The massive air conditioning systems installed outside were doing their best to extract the heat generated by thousands of whispering machines.

By dawn everything was up and running.

My rack didn't look nice or structured. The servers were all different: black, brown, white, metallic… Some were missing a lid. Cables routing was messy and labels were hand written instead of printed. I checked out other racks, they were fitted with the latest generation servers all from the same provider; usually HP or Dell. One particular rack contained only 2 Power Mac towers. It was the only one equipped with hardware from Apple.

At almost 7 in the morning, a dude arrived rushing. He was so agitated that he couldn't even find the key to open the secure door of his rack. He looked so devastated that I approached him to see what's going on. He showed me a wall of 1U servers with blue LEDs blinking in sync. They were connected to an impressive switch from Cisco.

The guy was just landing at Schiphol after he cancelled his holidays. All his boxes were rooted and the data destroyed. He explained that the machines were forming a cluster. Every server had *secure* certificates to connect to all other boxes without any password. Therefore, once the hackers gained access to the first machine, they went to all other without difficulty. I really felt for the poor bastard and in same time, this exposure was an eye opener about what could happen if I don't prepare for the unexpected.

Before leaving and just to put my mind at rest, I changed all passwords on my servers with stronger ones. Then, I went to Amsterdam city where I rented a bed in a cheap hotel smelling marijuana. I slept most of the day with the noise of thousands servers still echoing into my ears.

* * *

Surprisingly and as dodgy as it looked, my rack performed very well during the first few months and I was able to provide my customers with extra resources. The problem with my business model was the fact that successful websites needed more and more bandwidth and processing power to satisfy their audience. In a context where many competitors blatantly offered "unlimited" plans, I couldn't increase my prices to reflect the real resources usage. It was then a sort of race against the clock: I had to provision more and more hosting power at a constant price.

After weeks of migrations, all accounts were in my own racks. I shared images taken in the data center with my clients. For once, they were able to see physically the machines that hosted their projects. This reinforced my credibility as a full blown host and not only someone reselling services acquired in various places.

The demand was high and many clients needed entry level dedicated servers to develop their websites even further. Again, I went to eBay but this time, I wasn't keen to build my own machines. Searching for a few hours, I found some old HP Compaq Proliant 360 for about 100 Euros each. They were used indeed, but that was the same hardware that used to sell for 3000 Euros just a few years earlier. I thought that for the price, nothing could go wrong.

I purchased 10 Proliants and a couple of IBMs Netfinity 4000. They all had SCSI drives, dual power supplies, multiple network adapters, hardware RAID and many other exciting features in just a 1U chassis.

My problems started when I received the shipment. I couldn't install my usual CentOS Linux on the HPs. The firmware of the RAID card was so old that the operating system was unable to detect any storage device. I spent more than a week playing with pages of BIOS settings and trying different Linux distributions in order to get anything to work in there.

I attempted to get some assistance from HP but I quickly realized that original manufacturers are allergic to people who buy their hardware on eBay, car boot sales or flea markets. For them, if it doesn't come from an approved retailer and with proper maintenance contracts, they don't support it. To make the situation worse, many tools, knowledge base articles and firmwares are not publicly available but restricted to their support personnel and approved customers.

I lost two weeks dealing with these servers in one side and trying to win some time with my impatient customers in other side. Eventually, I managed to make 8 servers out of 10 work. The other 2, I used them as parts and spares.

The machines from IBM never worked. Basically they don't have keyboard, monitor or mouse ports as we know them. There is just one single flat connector that needs special adapter cable. I emailed the seller but I received the classic canned response: *"If it's not specified in the auction, it's not there. And, by the way, don't assume anything in the future."*

Worldwide, there was only one single Netfinity KVM cable for sale. It was in the US with a seller who wasn't thrilled to ship abroad. After negotiations, I paid more than the price of the servers to get this bloody cable shipped to me by UPS.

I paid again for a boring travel back to Amsterdam in order to deploy this hardware and perform other maintenance tasks.

When I returned home, I started sending access credentials and getting money in exchange. It wasn't big money as we are talking about entry level boxes. All the hassle was to receive 20 or 25 Euros per month per machine.

I needed 6 months of continuous operations to pay for all the fees and break even. Then, all the money would have been considered as benefit. In fact, six months later, all these servers were in the big electronic rubbish container in the parking lot of the data center.

The law of series started with one HP server that failed and refused to boot. As I couldn't travel to Amsterdam for just that incident, I gave my customer the credentials for another server. Luckily, he had an up to date backup so he was online in no time. A week later, another customer reported similar issue. Again, after several reboots, I had to give him another machine. At the third incident, I started worrying and removed remaining Proliants from my offer. To be in the safe side, I asked my other customers using similar boxes to schedule an offsite backup every 12 hours until I found out what the problem was. I wasn't finding out. Without the OEM support, there was no way for me to understand or fix the problem.

When I had the money to pay for another travel to Amsterdam, half of the servers were in the dark. In fact, the money collected wasn't to "pay for another travel"! It was to pay my bills, my food and other living expenses. However, the irony was that every time I managed to get some money in my bank account, a new emergency arose and forced me to spend it.

I opened the rack and connected a monitor to the first server. Apparently, all the data was corrupted. A faulty RAID card was my prime suspect. There was nothing I could do. It would have been pure madness to reformat and use again a server who corrupted the data in a mysterious incident. In fact, in all the servers seemed to have suffered the same fate. My only option was to discard them all, including the ones that weren't rented out yet. For the good measure, I also put the old IBMs on the bin even if they didn't have shown any issue at that time.

My reputation didn't improve with these multiple incidents. I tried to go to a niche no one wanted: entry level servers. There was a little or no money there but only big risks to take. My ratio risk/revenue was too unfavorable. I am not even surprised that I hit the wall.

Don't get me wrong here: when new and properly maintained, HP and IBM servers are really good. Actually the World Wide Web runs on this sort of machines. I already logged in to some with more than 700 days of continuous uptime. But when their useful life is over and are given to electronic waste recyclers to dispose of, don't even try to give them another go. If they have been deemed unfit for production, it was for good reasons. After many years operating at full potential, they were typically entering in a red area where failure is a norm.

My troubles didn't seem to end. Do you remember the Baytech power switches I told you about before? They started losing their IP addresses. For some reason, they seemed to forget everything and revert to default factory settings. I was unable to connect remotely and reboot my servers when they crash. Data center Technicians charged 100 Euros for each reboot and – even for that price – sometimes it took them 12 hours just to acknowledge my request. I couldn't afford the fees and the downtime. Again I jumped in the train for Amsterdam to find a solution.

I took the first Baytech and connected it via serial cable to a Windows server. This switch was controlling power plugs for other servers but not that particular Windows. Therefore, if any server crashed, I could login to the Windows, then go to the console of the power switch and reboot. The power plug for that Windows server was connected to another Baytech itself connected to a Linux server via a serial port again... This hack worked for me but I couldn't give access to individual ports to my customers. The loss of this feature wasn't popular.

My first generation of handmade servers started showing some signs of wear. Most of them were built out of desktop PCs hardware. They are not designed, meant or supposed to run 24 hours a day at full load. Submitted to this regime, my machines started crashing on regular basis. Some crashed once a month, other once a week and a few more frequently than that.

Murphy's Law being what it is, it was only when I was enjoying a dinner with friends, attending a Doctor appointment or trying to sleep that crashes occurred the most. I can't tell how many times I came back home to find my inbox full of emails from customers complaining about their server "down" again.

I remember one particular machine that used to crash every night randomly between 1 to 5 AM. It kept me sleep deprived for a couple of weeks the time for me to replace it. I put a mattress near my desk and I used to get up every 20 minutes to check if it was online. Then when the nightly crash occurred, I power cycled it then I was safe to sleep for some hours.

Multiple small incidents took their toll from my customers' patience. I was alternating between short times where I could make some money in excess of my immediate needs, to times where I had to withdraw everything to cover for incidents.

Anytime my account went north of 2000 Euros, I felt nervous because I knew that an Armageddon was coming to collect the money. It never failed to materialize.

I remember when I lost my most important customer. He was paying nearly 200 Euros/month for a server and wanted to upgrade to a solution in the area of 400 Euros a month. I could almost pay my flat rental just with that customer but I had to keep him satisfied at any cost.

His request to upgrade arrived as good news after a few high profile incidents and the loss of some serious customers. He needed to host one single website that received a lot of hits and distributed multimedia content. I knew that he needed a fast disks array regardless of anything else. There is no point of adding more CPUs and more memory if the data is ultimately read from a single miserable hard drive.

For him, the ideal solution would have been a RAID 10 with 4 large drives. I had the money to buy 2 drives only. Even after slashing my food budget, I couldn't afford more. In the meantime, the customer was pushing for a faster server and I didn't want him to go somewhere else.

I promised that the box will be ready over the weekend and I took the train to Amsterdam. In my bag, I had a sandwich and 2 disks only.

Once in the data center, I pulled my best server ever: a 2U machine with 4 Xeon processors and 16 Gb of ECC RAM. It was considered as a beast at the time. I installed the 2 disks in there and started the configuration page for the RAID controller. It gave me the safe low performance choice: RAID1 and the unthinkable RAID 0. With RAID 0 the data is stripped across the disks which give higher performance. But if any disk fails, all the data is permanently lost!

At the time, my latest disk failure occurred more than a year ago. I swear to God that I never tried to compromise on disks quality. I always purchased the high-end ones guaranteed 5 years by their manufacturers. They are usually meant for Enterprise production environment. I enforced this policy because I knew that it was so difficult for me to handle a disk failure by travelling to Netherlands at the moment notice.

After a silent prier, I decided to take the risk and go for RAID 0. I felt taking a calculated risk as most disks don't fail during their life time. Also, my idea was to wait for the customer to pay a month or two then use the money to buy more hard drives for him and upgrade him to fast and safe RAID 10. I wanted the RAID 0 to cover me just during that short time.

When the machine was ready, I sent the credentials to the customer. He was really happy with the performance and immediately started moving his data.

Three weeks went on without any incidents. My number of orders decreased but I was working frantically to stabilize my servers and respond to support tickets almost in real time. I wanted the satisfaction rate to increase because this is the only way to keep current customers and get referral for more business.

It was a Friday early afternoon and I was at my 50th email already: renewing domains, resetting passwords, chasing for payments, sending quotes… when a new email sent an electric shock down my spine: a server, the one with RAID 0 disks, stopped responding. The customer wasn't worried at all. He just dropped a line asking for a reboot as soon as possible. I responded immediately that his is issue is being taken care of and logged in to my Windows server, then to the Baytech console to reset the power.

Once I've done that, I checked my watch. Normally, if everything goes well, I should be able to see the SSH login prompt within 5 to 10 minutes. I waited nervously counting the seconds. I knew that with my basic contract with the data center, my SLA was defined as *"Best Effort"*. This means no SLA at all. As it was Friday, any ticket from me would have been answered on Monday at the earliest.

Half an hour later and even after a couple of more hard resets, the server was still offline. I quickly prepared a small bag with some tools, the keys for the racks, some rescue CDs and a tooth brush.

I informed the customer that something wrong happened with the server and that *"our technicians"* were doing their best to fix it. Our technicians were me running to the train station while holding my pants like a First World War solider running to the front.

By the way, let me make another confidence. During that time as a sole trader, I suffered a multiple personalities syndrome. I used to work days and nights and trying to sleep when I could. One day, a customer noticed that pattern and asked me if I was alone in the company. He was a high maintenance guy that used to log tickets on daily basis at different times. I felt a little bit exposed because I wanted to give the public the perception that my company was large enough. For some reason – maybe I was right, maybe I was wrong – I had the feeling that people wouldn't trust my business had they knew that the whole show was being run by a single person. I also wanted to avoid people discovering that I was what I really was: a no life. It wasn't by choice but I had no other option than fighting online saving my life a Paypal at a time.

In the next few days, I invented Mike, John, Pascal and even Cynthia. In case someone was trying to study their patterns, I created a rotational weekly schedule for each of them. Everyone was using a personalized email address and a customized signature to answer at specific times of the day.

One of the most feared personalities was *"Pascal"* the Accountant. He had all power to keep records in good standing including disconnecting servers and shutting down accounts. He was feared like the Abominable Snowman. Any time I cc'd him in an email, an aura of fear floated in the air. Many customers who were dying in intensive care, in prison, or attending the fifth funeral of their grandma released the money without further questions.

Back to Amsterdam: I arrived at Schiphol late evening with one of the latest trains. The place was deserted apart from a group of jetlagged tourists sleeping on the floor.

I took a free shuttle that goes from the airport main building to the long term parking a couple of miles away. Then, I resumed running for an hour or so until I reached the World-Class Data Center.

Nervously, I opened my rack. The box that caused all the havoc was there with a red light blinking. Through the deafening noise of thousands other servers, I could hear distinctly the alarm bell of its RAID card. I hooked an old Sony monitor to the VGA port and started some diagnostic tests. The failure I feared the most, the failure that I couldn't afford at that particular moment happened. One disk was dead.

I removed the hard drive, gave it a good shake, a couple of hits in the side and placed it back. Don't laugh; it's the only thing you can attempt in such situations. Sometime, I say sometimes, it may give it a new run. It didn't work for me.

Inspecting my other boxes, I found a machine that I stopped a few days ago after terminating the contract of a non-paying customer. I scavenged the hard drives. They were much smaller than what I needed, but I had no other choice. I put them on the server I was repairing, set the RAID level to 1 and booted on a CD. It took me a couple of hours to install CentOS Linux and all the software needed for hosting.

When I sent the credentials of the server to the client, it was 2 AM. At the time, he was down for more than 12 hours and not happy at all. My relief was very short lived. Within 5 minutes, he responded to my email: *"The server is up but empty now. Where is my data? Are you going to restore the data now?"* I put just one interrogation mark here but in the original message there were half a dozen of them.

After some back and forth, he explained that the server was used for everything including development and storing backups. No complete and up to date copies of the data existed anywhere else. You wouldn't believe how many companies don't have even a basic disaster recovery strategy. I had the habit to give free FTP accounts to my customers to use as repositories for backup storage. Most of them never bothered to consider them.

I felt sorry for him but also sorry for myself as I was clearly going to lose an important account again. I was stuck in a vicious cycle: technical solutions to provide top level service were available but I couldn't afford them with what my customers was paying. In other hand, I couldn't increase my prices because my reputation was in decline due to all the incidents accumulated in a short period of time. Something else was hitting hard: the overselling. More and more companies were offering plans with: *unlimited* bandwidth, *unlimited* storage, and *unlimited* domain names hosting for 99 cents per month. Some of them were pushing even further by offering a *lifetime* everything unlimited hosting for a single payment. These companies were indeed lying and misrepresenting the product. There is no disk with unlimited capacity and no network port with unlimited debit. If they were telling the truth, they could've hosted eBay, Google and Youtube in the same time. Their hosting had a lot of hidden limits. One of their favorite is to restrict the size and the number of requests or open connections to the MySQL database. As most websites rely on MySQL, this means that the hosting plan is useless for most projects. To sustain their prices, they had to squeeze up to 2000 websites in a single server. I used to host from 50 to 150 websites per machine depending on its specifications. When a customer start using too much of the "unlimited" resources, they just found a pretext and shut his website down without any compensation. Usually they pretext some mysterious breach of their sacred Terms of Service to terminate the account

I don't believe that these hosts with their unscrupulous methods were doing any serious money. Many were opening, many were closing or changing names but no one showed any sign of success. However, they were killing the market by driving prices down, selling at loss and giving the customer the feeling that everything should be unlimited when it comes to web hosting.

After a few more emails with the customer, he confirmed that he was leaving. There was nothing I could do to prevent that.

I went to the lobby of the data center. A security agent was slumping in his chair while watching night programs on television. No one else was in the building. I took all the change I had and went to a vending machine to buy some biscuits. I felt hungry and defeated.

Upstairs there were a couple of small sofas in a hallway. I pushed them close to each other and decided to have a nap. I couldn't turn the harsh neon light off or do anything about the air-conditioning that was chilling the air. I managed to sleep a couple of hours in a very uncomfortable position. Later when I opened my eyes, it was bright outside. I went to the servers' room to check my emails on a Windows 2003 box: we may never know; maybe good news. No; no good news. Just a couple of emails about lost passwords and other trivial questions. But it was time to start my long walk to the airport.

After countless hours jumping from a train to another, I arrived home feeling more tired and miserable than ever but my day wasn't over. Before even taking a shower, I had to login to my systems and see if there were any issues, tickets or complaints during my absence.

On the support forum, dozens of people were online which was highly unusual. My email client, Thunderbird, announced more than 100 new emails before they started downloading.

Bad news: my day wasn't over.

44

Hacked Server

I didn't have to read the integrality of new emails to understand what was going on. Many of my customers were complaining about the same thing. All pages, whether static HTML or dynamic PHP, were modified and a malicious code added to them. This code displayed ads, opened pop-ups and triggered antivirus alerts to their visitors. One server was concerned: my most important one! It hosted almost 150 websites distributing many thousands pages of content. All of them were infected.

It wasn't time to cry or kill myself. I had to fight again if I wanted to eat and keep a roof over my head. I posted a one liner in the forum *"we are investigating"* then I logged in to the server. At least 5 or 6 hackers were happily connected as root.

I had to act very quickly. If I lost that machine, that same day I would have had to close my business.

I changed the root password; it took me 20 seconds. Then, I went to the network configuration file and changed the IP of the server; 30 seconds more. Then, I configured the SSH to accepted logons from only one single IP in the world. It was the IP of a Windows 2003 server based in the same data center. This took me another 20 seconds. Then, I logged in to the power switch and cut the power on the hacked server.

I left it down for an hour or so just to mislead the attackers to believe that it was brought offline permanently. Then, I applied the power and the server came back online but under a different IP address. I still kept Apache down so no website was displayed which reinforced the idea that the box was still offline.

In web support web forum, I told my customers that "we" were moving the data to a new machine. It wasn't true because I hadn't any machine ready for that and all websites were corrupted. However, I had to lie just in case the attacker was an insider.

I contacted a developer I used to chat with online. I knew him just by his nickname. He was also a no life spending all his time online for some obscure activities. Nobody else could help me out but him.

I provided him with a sample of a hacked page and what I needed: a program that can find all the pages hosted on the server and restore them to their original form by removing the malicious code. The only thing that saved me that day is the fact that the pirates didn't destroy the data but added their junk to it.

During the night, I received my program and ran it in the server. It took it a few hours to clean everything. In the meantime, I updated all the software and removed all malicious tools that were installed in various locations. My solution wasn't orthodox as it's always recommended to format the server and start from scratch in such situations. But clearly, I couldn't do that and say good-by to all my users.

By dawn, all pages were up, clean and running again. It was a big success, but still I had to compensate some vocal customers just to buy their silence and keep them in my network.

Against all rules and all odds, I managed to keep the server online for a month without any further incident. It took me that time to spare some money to pay for another trip to Amsterdam to prepare a new server where I moved all the accounts out of the hacked box.

During my years as a fulltime webhost, I used to run Linux and Windows servers. Both operating systems were facing the same public network and used for similar projects. All my servers were maintained and secured at the same frequency.

While many people think that Linux is more secure than Windows, I have to admit that 100% of my security incidents involved Linux only. In my entire career no one ever breached to even a single Windows machine.

The last paragraph wasn't sponsored by Microsoft.

The Coyote Group

Ask any sole trader, they all have the same secret dream: a big customer with a lot of money bringing a deal that could send the business into orbit. I used to believe in that like some teen girls keep a dream of a charming Prince on a white horse.

Before going any further, I would like you to read and think about the different between these two emails:

Email one:

Hello, please provide a quote for 8 servers, 4 CPU (Xeon/Opteron mid-range), 16 Gb RAM (ECC preferred), RAID 10 SATA 2 Tb total is a must. Traffic expected circa 2 Tb/box/month. Ready to go on yearly contract if good incentive.

Please write or call if you need any further details.

Thank you

Email two:

Hello, we would like to host our project and don't know the requirements. We need a detailed quote from you. Our website will host videos. We will have paid and free accounts with different options and levels of service. We don't have an estimation of the number of users, but we can set the up the bar at 100'000 users to start with.

In the first email, the customer knows what he needs and seems keen on details. I would take time to call him or exchange some emails to build a relationship before talking money. If you provide figures immediately, you will be selected on price only. It means that if any competitor provides a lower quote, he will win the deal. You don't want that. That's why it's important to create a relationship. When the customer gets to know you, he is more likely to perceive other values and stay with you even if you are not the cheapest provider. Competing on price only is the worst thing you can do. You can get as low as you want, there will be always someone else who is ready to sell for a dollar less. Some can even sell at loss.

If you want to be the "Easyjet" of your field, you are going to wipe out your bank account and realize it when your debit card is refused at a petrol station. I for one don't give any sort of credit to this sort of projects when started by a sole trader.

Back to our emails: the first message is from someone you can reasonably hope to make business with. The second message, if someone ever dares to send it to me, I will chase him with a hunting rifle loaded with salt and pepper.

If you read between the lines, the email has been written by someone who doesn't even know the size of his project and its technical requirements. It means he didn't work on a business plan; therefore he doesn't have the money.

At this phase of his project, it's too early for him to ask for a "quote". What he needs, is a Consultant who can work with him to define his project from the technical point of view. Only when his solution is well defined on the paper, then he can try to get some quotes.

This feasibility study is expensive to realize but it's unavoidable for anyone who wants to have the slightest chance to succeed.

When I was a sole trader, I have been literally abused by people hiding a genuine feasibility study inside a fake quote request. I used to spend days searching, testing and calibrating to answer the 1 million-dollar question: *"what do they need for this project?"* Then I would send my *"technical offer"* with all the details and my pricing. Usually, they would keep just the technical details and use them to shop around from other suppliers.

Much later, when I realized the pattern, I moved to a more professional approach: you have a project but you don't know how many servers and what software you need? You want to know what would be the size of your infrastructure for 1000, 10'000 and 100'000 users? I can answer that for $2000.

Oh, it's too expensive? Let me help you out: if you use me as main supplier for your servers, I would give you a $2000 cash-back. So the technical study would be free at the end of the day!

Oh, you have no money for the study now? Welcome to the club bro. Welcome to a world of pain. We are all after money we don't own currently.

* * *

I was in a very bad mood counting my losses of the previous month when I received an email from a customer. He needed a quote for a massive infrastructure he considered to move to my network. He explained that his start-up launched a couple of years ago a sort of images hosting service. It was based on a model of free users with paid upgrade options.

According to him, they had already accumulated millions of hosted items and wanted to expand. They weren't satisfied with their current solution and wanted to swap for something bigger, faster and were ready to spend more indeed.

Reading his signature, the name wasn't unheard of. I checked my files and I found that this guy had already a couple of personal websites with me. They were both on a server that never crashed or slowed down since its installation. I figured out that he was so happy that he decided to refer me to his start-up.

After a couple of emails, I felt like hitting the jackpot. I wouldn't find it unbelievable that he was also asking other supplies for quotes, but I was ready to work hard to win that deal at any cost. It was a matter of death or life for my business.

He didn't share with me the name of his company but it didn't bother me at that stage of the negotiations. However, I used the figures he gave me as intelligence to try to identify the company by doing some searches online. It was obvious that they were definitely in the top 10 images hosts. I studied the profile of every single company to make sure I know them all and I understand how they work. I printed a shortlist of web URLs and attached in the wall in front of my desk. The client who was knocking at my door was in that list. Time will tell which one is he.

I spent the first week elaborating a document detailing the IT infrastructure needed to host the project: servers, load balancers, firewalls, switches, cables… To avoid quoting too low then blowing up the budget, I decided to include everything in my document. Even the square screws to fix the servers to the racks were included.

My initial solution was based on 30 servers. Some were hosting the website itself while other stored the files. I submitted the quote to the customer for review. He came back and said that they wanted two separate networks with different level of performance. Their aim was to create separate zones for free and paying customers. The idea wasn't totally absurd but it needed a lot more servers. We were looking at 50 machines when I submitted the amended solution.

Another set of changes was demanded. The customer requested different processors, insisted on having a different network configuration, changing RAID levels… It was still reasonable for a project of that size but we were already one month down the line.

When I started placing prices near the items, the final cost went quickly to 5 digits then jumped to 6 when the Cisco equipment was thrown in.

These numbers were screaming something: this project was just too big for me.

I couldn't realistically launch something of that dimension while I wasn't even sure to afford my next ticket to the data center. I had to find a partner with enough credentials to make this happens. I asked my customer to allow me a couple of more days and contacted Rackspace. I had a lot of respect for this company because they started in a garage to grow to one of the most successful IT and hosting companies.

They responded to my enquiry very quickly and one of their employees, a lady actually, was happy to board a flight from London to meet with me and my customer to discuss the project. It's totally normal and very usual for smaller businesses to use larger ones as partners in situations like this one. I have already seen a 100-employees strong company working with bigger players to deliver a project larger than their current financial and logistical capabilities.

With the help of Rackspace and before any face to face meeting, I managed to bring the conversation back in tracks with my prospect. Suddenly, I felt that after all what I have done I was entitled to know everything including the name his company.

I didn't want to involve Rackspace personnel any further without having all cards in hand. I called my customer and I explained that at such an advanced stage, he needed to release the name of his start-up for us to know whom we are working with. For his peace of mind, I offered to sign a non-disclosure agreement.

Carefully, like a teenage girl admitting the name of her first boyfriend he decided to tell me everything.

- Well, our start-up is the Coyote Group

By the time he finished this first sentence, I was lying on the floor like struck by a non-magmatic meteorite. In fact, I worked so intensively that there was nothing I didn't know about the image hosting market. If the so called "Coyote Group" wasn't in my list, it meant that it didn't exist.

I felt my blood pressure dropping. My only hope was that sometimes the legal and the public name of the business are not the same. But still, I never heard about the Coyote Group. I asked him to drop me and email with the website address and hanged up.

When I received the URL, it just confirmed my fear. It was a long and unpronounceable domain name that was registered just a few months ago. The website itself was empty apart from a short form to upload images. A few minutes later, I found how to browse the content of the server to see how many images have been ever uploaded. There were like 10 or 12 generic landscapes and Windows desktop backgrounds probably placed there to test the upload script.

I was physically sick. More than a month of hard work went down the drain. My prospect had no project and no budget. For some reasons that only a Neo-Freudian Psychiatrist can comprehend, this person felt fulfilled and gratified by having people working on fantasies.

While wasting my time on this illusion, I had less energy and resources spent on marketing. I was even slower supporting my regular customers. I realized that it might be the hit too much.

I asked my contact at Rackspace to cancel any arrangements for travel and close the case. I explained how my prospect led me to believe on a big project that existed only in his impaired brain.

As we were heading towards the end of the month, I emailed the data center to give notice of cancellation for one of my racks. The termination of the contract would have been effective only at the end of the following month, but it was at least a move to lower my monthly bills. It wasn't a strategic choice but an obligation to avoid filing for bankruptcy.

I learnt many lessons from this incident. The first one is to never work more than an hour to provide a quote. If the elaboration of the estimate requires answering any complex questions, then a consulting service must be billed. If the customer is not willing to pay for the consulting, then ask him to reformulate his quotation request and provide himself a detailed break-up of all what he needs.

Another lesson I would like to share with you also: anyone prospecting for deal significantly larger than your average customer, is probably a time waster. Imagine you are a restaurant owner who sells pizzas for $10 to $20. Do you think that some of your customers can afford a helping of Iranian Beluga caviar at $500? I am sure some of them do. Now, ego put a side, how many would buy caviar in your restaurant? Certainly no one! There is a reason behind that: the way your present your business, the way you set your prices and market your products define you. The day you place a $10 pizza in your menu, you implicitly renounce to sell caviar for $500. People still buy it, but not from you.

When you sell cheap items, even if you are excellent at what you do, clients wouldn't trust you for much more expensive products. That's why when some big brands want to sell more affordable item, they create a sub-brand to do that. Otherwise, they would lose their credibility in their core market.

The difference between a small business and a major corporation in terms of market position is the following: big players decide almost scientifically in which segment of the market they want to place their products and services. The small business in other hand let the market defines him. A sole trader – for instance – tries various strategies until he finds a position where for some obscure reasons he seems to fit. Then he will be a prisoner for that segment. Any attempt to go higher or lower would invariably fail.

If I had to do it again, I would spend months just analyzing the market until I get an intimate knowledge about all my competitors and their respective positions in market spectrum (I just invented this concept of "market spectrum", but it sounds too good). This would be my first priority before doing anything else.

Well, with the "Coyote Group" I got carried away but I learnt the lessons I am sharing with you here. I threatened the customer to bill the time invested on his non-existing project but I knew that without a contract, I had only myself to blame. He didn't respond to my emails or return my calls after that. He then disappeared from the place and I never heard from him again.

However, my small business took a serious blow. I spent a month consolidating my hosting in fewer servers then I closed a rack. The decision was taken just in time! Because a month later, I had in my bank account just enough money to pay for one single rack. I would have defaulted otherwise!

Using virtualization, I manage to increase the density of my hosting. I mean I was able to put more accounts per machine in order to make it financially viable for me. This helped me a lot as I realized that when they are properly maintained and managed, my machines were able to deliver more power and host more customers. It wasn't only the servers, it was me: I was getting better in my job. I was able to fix and secure Linux like never before. Finished were the sleepless nights monitoring MySQL to restart if it crashed! I created scripts and programs that did some of my job for me. With that same knowledge, I could have been in position to make millions a few years before. But it was late; almost too late.

Desperate Measures

I received a letter. The kind of letters you don't like: gray, ugly and bearing my full name as in my birth certificate; official; very official: the Tax Office. They were not happy at all.

In fact, when my business gained momentum, I hired a local accountant to validate my financial records and prepare my company tax returns. As long as he was doing the job, I used to pay a little or no tax. In most countries a sole trader can remove many of his spending from his revenue. When working from home, even part of the rental can be tax free. However, when things went in a downfall spiral, I had to cut costs. My priorities were to keep the servers online and myself alive. Everything else had to go.

Since I terminated my contract with the Accountant, my financial records were in a state of advanced mess. It went to the point where I couldn't honestly say who paid and who didn't. Many clients noticed some leniency in my management and started dodging their bills. They were playing for time to pay as late as possible or to skip payments.

I remember a particular client who was writing almost on daily basis to complain about his dedicated server. The machine was online and working just fine but he always found a tiny detail to log a complaint about. It was getting so ridiculous that I spoke about with my aunt. She had no technical knowledge about servers but she found an interesting anomaly in that scenario:

- Why would someone who is apparently so unhappy with the service still stay with you month after month and not leaving for another supplier?

Nice one isn't it? I opened my books and logged in to my company bank account to do some math. After many checks, I realized that he didn't pay for 6 consecutive months! Due to a flaw in my accounting methodology, he managed to slip through the net.

When I challenged him about the payments, he sent me a condescending email explaining that "as matter of rule" he never pay bill before the end of the month and therefore I had to wait two weeks to see the money. Five minutes later, his server was in the dark. I hated pulling the plug on production servers as it went against the vision I had on my job and my duties. I tried to follow a sort of "intelligent dispute resolution" but obviously you can't do that with stupid people.

The client was begging for the return of his server online. He explained that his web agency was going to cease business if the outage lasts for longer. Then, he sent a Paypal covering one month to "prove his good faith" and asked for 24 hours grace delay to prepare the funds and pay the remainder.

I had no professional or personal interest in killing his business. My goal was to recover unpaid bills not to cause unnecessary damage. I brought his server online again and gave him the delay he requested.

A couple of days later, not seeing any money, I sent him a reminder. He didn't respond. I went again to the server and cut the power. However, when I visited his website, it was still online. A ping confirmed that he profited from the payment delay to move his data and customers to another provider.

He never responded to my further emails or paid the outstanding bills. I contacted a debt collection agency, but they asked me for an upfront payment without any guarantee that they could "haul the money". With my declining funds, the battle wasn't affordable.

Since then, anytime I had to shut down an unpaid service, I would never restore it. The only time I made an exception it was when a customer died of cancer and I gave back the unpaid server to his son in order for him to prevent the collapse of the family business. I am not a monster after all.

* * *

The letter from the Tax Office contained a bad news for me. As my last tax return – that was filled late – was incorrect and incomplete, they decided to hit me with a settlement figure of their own. They wanted 4000 Euros. In fact, that year I was so broke that even 10 Euros would have been unfair. With a proper Accountant and clean records, I would have been able to pay nothing or even claim money from them. But it wasn't time for discussion.

All my fortune at the time was 1500 Euros at the bank and some loose change in a jar. To avoid further fines and escalation, I wired all what I had to the taxman then I wrote a letter asking for more time to pay the rest by installments.

A couple of days later, a customer whom I befriended called to offer a deal: *"we need to send 15 million emails mate! It's for a casino"* I told to him that it was not something I could consider as my servers would be shut down within hours if I start mass emailing.

No data center managers would close your servers if they receive one or two complaints about you. The bigger customer you are, the more complaints you can get away with. If you have a virtual server at $10 dollars you would be taken offline if your provider receives a couple of abuse reports the same month. But if you have some expensive servers running they know that you are hosting a lot of websites and the likelihood of incidents is potentially higher. Usually if your respond quickly and take prompt action when they contact you following incidents, you keep good standing in the house.

However, sending millions of emails was out of question. That would cause thousands of complaints and the termination of my contract with the data center.

In other hand, the business wasn't doing well and I was understandably low on cash. At that time I was even cutting on essential spending like food and health. I couldn't possibly miss a deal. My friend told me that the customer provisioned 2000 Euros of budget for the "right person" and was open to pay more if needed.

I wasn't seduced by the offer but I was tempted. However I needed to know more before taking any decision. My friend explained with his eternal cheerful and optimistic pitch: *"Look, I am here with the Project Manager and I am impressed by the degree of preparation of this enterprise. Everything is going to work flawlessly!"* For some reason, I felt that my friend was bullshitting his prospect. He had serious issues with money and many people were looking for him in various countries in Europe for different debts he never paid. He never accepted the idea that he owed anything to anyone. For him, all these stories were just about some speculative joint-ventures that didn't work as expected and his associates lost their invested money. As some business lawyers like to say: bad management is not a crime.

He explained that the emails contain an advertisement about a casino and an affiliation link. For every customer who registers via the link and download the gaming software, they would receive $10 commission.

- Then, imagine if only 1% of people who receive our emails go to the casino website and download the software! That's 10'000 new users per million emails. For us, it's $100'000 per million emails and we sending 15 million of them! We can't fail!

I couldn't believe what I was hearing. I suspected him to be serious. He sounded so enthusiastic that he certainly believed in his foolish prediction. I for one never accept money from people if I can't give them genuine value for it. I had to make sure they were aware that they were going to hit the wall.

Trying to sound as professional as possible, I explained that the conversion ratio they were contemplating was overly optimistic. I also explained that the spam filters are so elaborated that most emails would never reach their target. When I finished talking, I heard this:

- Look, anyway, if we don't get 1% conversion, we would get 1/1000 in worst case scenario. That's still ten grand per million emails.

- Are you conscious that your conversion rate can be even lower than 1/1000?

- Yes we are but we think that it does worth the try

- Ok then, when do you want to start?

- Immediately. We can send a Western Union this afternoon.

That day, I spent hours searching for "bullet proof" and "bulk email friendly" servers. There are no serious, scrupulous and reputable providers in this market. However, there are many fly-by-night and scammers ready to take your dollars then slam the door in your face.

To avoid any misunderstanding, I made it clear with my customer that I can't offer any warranty that the job will be completed as he desired. He was paying me to try, not to succeed. It may sound weird when we are used to contracts based on results. But here, there was no contract apart from the given parole that I will do my best.

I found a supplier in Panama. The website looked as dodgy as it gets. They promised a Linux server with mailing software and rotating IP addresses. They never used the word "free to spam" but it was strongly implied. I also discovered a couple of similar offers in Hong-Kong and Russia but sounded even less credible.

That day, I went to a Western Union to receive my cash. I sent half of it to Panama and kept the other half: it was my share.

Back home, I created an FTP account for my friend to upload his emails addresses. Even if he trusted me, I asked him to create a few dozens of email accounts and include them randomly in the lists he provides me with. These addresses are unknown to me and would act as probes to give him hard evidence that his emails have been dispatched.

Whenever I am maneuvering in a gray area, I prefer to take the initiative and give my partners all possible venues to feel comfortable. It's not only in their best interest, but also in mine. When the deal is risky, there is a high probability that things go wrong and you would have to justify and answer many questions. For this reason, it's important to think ahead and prepare in advance the cards you would show in case of crappy outcome.

I quickly received the files. There were 150 of them each containing between 80'000 to 120'000 email addresses. Apparently they were purchased from someone who attested that all these people – the equivalent of all the population of Netherlands – agreed, or opted-in, to receive marketing campaigns. I read through them randomly. Some seemed totally fabricated and some must have been grabbed online by some emails extractor script.

Well, let's be realistic here, if these emails were legitimate, I wouldn't have been sending cash to Panama.

After a few hours of sleep, I got up and walked to my computer. I always left my machine running days and nights for it to be ready at the moment notice. I used to reboot it once ever few weeks or when my tired Windows showed its dismissive blue screen of death. When you work 16 hours a day, every minute counts.

The email from the Panamanians was there. I immediately logged in to the control panel of the machine. It was built to do only one thing: sending bulk emails.

I uploaded my first list and started spamming while drinking a tea.

* * *

Next morning, sat at the same table, I was celebrating my first million emails sent. However, in terms of results, there was nothing to brag about. The statistics displayed by the server were much worse than the worst case scenario. In 100'000 messages, only 90 to 110 land in someone's inbox! The rest is blocked by anti-spam software. Then, for every 100 messages actually opened by the recipient, there are only 4 or 5 clicks to the casino link provided. How many clickers register and download the software? One in fifty only. Therefore, the conversion rate was roughly about 1 successful action per million emails sent. The client was clearly at loss. Misled by my friend, he was expecting a crazy ROI of $150'000 for just 2000 Euros invested. At the pace the story was going, he was set to get $150 out of his 2000 Euros.

To help them out, I decided to write the email myself. It was something more elaborated than *"Hey, click-here to make money quick"*. The sales pitch increased the conversation rate but still most emails were lost in the black hole of internet spam filters.

A few days later, while I was uploading a new list of emails, the server stopped responding. I called the supplier hot line. A guy with an American accent explained that the service was terminated and they keep all the money. Apparently, even if they had nothing against bulk emailing, they received too many complaints about my particular account. It's not unusual to get abuse reports on email marketing campaigns but I was well above the classic quota.

I remembered my friend telling me that the addresses belonged all to people who double opted-in to receive marketing material. I tried to explain that to the Support Agent but he didn't buy into that.

- Double opt-in you said? No way. You dispatched emails to domains that end with dot gov and dot edu. Do you think that Government agencies and top universities would accept casino bullshit from you?

The call then ended abruptly along with my short career as a professional spammer.

Understandably, the customer wasn't happy. He was even upset; not necessarily about me but with my friend who closed his Facebook account and went into the hiding.

I made enough money to survive another month and pay for my servers but I never felt the end so close.

* * *

Many sole traders and small businesses animate web forums to support their clients. What's good with that is - after a while - you get a lot of content and any customer before opening a support ticket can search in the forum and probably find the answer to his question. For you, it also serves as a knowledge base and you can refer users to any particular post relevant to their case. People can interact in a forum and help each other offloading your support. Then, with all the technical keywords in there, the forum can rank well with search engines and attract traffic...

With all that in mind, a support forum is a bad idea and my recommendation is to **not** to use it!

When I created my web hosting company, I immediately installed a forum. In the welcome email I used to send to every new client, I included a link and an invitation to join the forum for "faster support". Without realizing I opened a Pandora box that almost killed my business!

Something very fishy was happening in the background and I wasn't aware about it. Let me tell you how I discovered it.

A customer posted a support message in the forum complaining about MySQL showing *"too many connections"* and other errors. An hour later, he got impatient and updated the thread with something like: *"please respond to this asap!"* But the third message was even more interesting. It wasn't from the original poster but from someone with a new account responding to him: *"Oh look, the owner didn't login for 8 hours now. I don't think he will be responding to you. They are ignoring your messages"*.

Well when I arrived an found this, I promptly fixed the MySQL issue but I started digging to find who created this account and was using it to cause bad ambiance in the forum. As Administrator on SMF, I displayed that account and the IP used to register it. Then, I searched for all other accounts created with that same IP. I found 5 or 6 of them including a bona fide account belonging to a reseller! He was one of the most active members in the support forum. Basically he was logged in there 12 hours a day and 7 days a week! I went to the database and pulled the table with all private messages sent by him. I found that for almost a year he was engaging my customers via private messaging and providing a discount if they moved to his hosting service. Searching again, I found that another user was doing the same thing! Almost all customers I lost during the last 12 months went to these two bastards.

Two things hit me even more. These two guys, I met with them a few months earlier and invited them for a coffee. They were very friendly and nice with me. I was a million miles from thinking that they were screwing me in the back. The other thing is for all that time, no customer approached me to tell me what was happening. Many refused to go with them but no one had the idea to forward a message to me.

So be careful! If you use a forum to support your customers, you are sharing their details with the whole world to see. Anyone can target them and offer better deals or any other incentives to leave you.

Trust me on that: don't even think about using a web forum to support your customers for any online business!

Again, I was hit hard. Even if I chased the offenders from my network, they caused a profound damage difficult to assess.

Sponsoring & Charities

I used to receive like 2 or 3 sponsorship requests per week. People would contact me and ask for free hosting in exchange of some promotion. I used to ignore these requests until my business was successful enough that I had always plenty of spares resources to play with.

My first engagement was with a group of young lads who were already sponsored by Nintendo and other big names for a part of their activity. Good for me. I wanted to have my name in there too. I decided to accept their request and be a technical sponsor. I offered free hosting for the portal, the forum and the download server. In exchange, they were supposed to add my business to the list of their sponsors everywhere they appear.

I offered the hosting but when I checked later, I couldn't find any mention of my business. I contacted them and it took them about two days to respond. It was very unusual as they were responding within minutes during the negotiation phase. They told me that they were going to release a new version of their website and it is difficult for them to edit the current version to add my logo. Fair enough. I accepted this and was happily waiting for them to show my logo next of Nintendo's. In the meantime their pages were sucking bandwidth and using CPU like no tomorrow.

Six months later the new version was out. It looked sleek and professional and was even announced by many major gaming websites. All their sponsors and partners were listed but not my business. It was a little bit too much for me to handle. I was literally paying bandwidth surcharge to promote other brands!

That night, I sadly decided to pull the plug before going to sleep. The portal, the multi-thousand-member forum and everything else was in the dark. Game Over!

Next day I found a lot of emails from the webmasters. Full of promises as usual but I told them that I was out. Professional to the last minute, I created a backup of their data and put it online for them to download. Ten days later I checked, the website was still down. I never checked again and I believe that they never recovered. Some people prefer a loss-loss situation to any other venue.

The lesson I learnt here is again to have clear, timed and well defined agreements with people. What you do for me exactly? When? For how long are you going to do that? What do you need exactly in exchange of that? All these questions and their subtopics must be answered and agreed upon in writing before starting anything. Otherwise, your venture, agreement or whatever is doomed for failure.

Later I was contacted by a Christian community. They had a massive portal but they were struggling to host it. They wanted someone who could help and, in exchange, they would promote services within their members and other affiliates. It wasn't easy to host their content. They were attacked on regular basis and I had to spend sleepless nights hardening the server and analyzing miles of ever growing log files. However, the whole experience was very rewarding. I received a lot of customers from them. Some weeks I got one customer a day! I also received envelopes with cash from well-wishers willing to help to keep the website online.

I hosted the website for a year and a half. After this time, it was so successful that it outgrew my hosting capacities. It needed more and more bandwidth half of which was wasted on denial of service attacks. The money and the leads I received were not even remotely enough to offset the actual cost of the hosting. As I was doing regular online meetings with the webmasters, they followed the evolution and were well aware of the situation. Eventually, after some repetitive crashes, they found someone who decided to finance a big server for them. Well, I could have provisioned myself such a server had they asked me. But it never crossed their minds. Why in your opinion? Think about it before reading any further.

Well, there are two different mindsets: free versus paid. I pay. I get this for free. These two mindsets are mutually exclusive. They cannot coexist both in the same time and you can't turn one into another. Think about it if you want to offer your services for free! When you work for free, people put the label *"free"* on your person. Sometimes it's not even conscious. They do it without realizing they are doing it but once you are labeled as a *"free"* person, they never pay you. I will tell you later a story were I helped to establish a business and worked my ass out for months and when the money came in, they hired people to do my job.

Anyway, the website left to a dedicated server somewhere else but it didn't survive. More than a server, it needed the technical commitment and countless administration hours I brought to it all the time it was growing. It saddened me sincere when they had to close it and break the vibrant community behind it but there was nothing I could do to reverse the sense of History.

I have seen so many successful websites closing because of their success! If you create an online project, you have to think very early about the monetization. How are you going to transform your traffic in money in order for you to – at least – sustain your technical costs? For ecommerce it's not an issue usually. Unless you have thousands of people just visiting but no one buying. For community websites, charities and no profit, the issue is real. You can host your website when it has 10, 100 or even 1000 visitors a day, but what would happen if the success is here and you need two massive servers and a full time Technical Administrator to keep them healthy and online? Many of my customers couldn't afford the technical bill because there was no clear monetization plan in place.

The Final Slump

More than half of my servers were down; some because I couldn't find any customer for them. Other failed at some point and I couldn't afford to repair them. All my money was going to pay for data center bills and taxes. In the same time, customers were more and more demanding. The old days of the dedicated server were slowly coming to an end. Everyone wanted to host in the "cloud". This vague and irritating world designates an installation with no single point of failure. It's usually based on diskless servers connected via fiber redundant paths to a data storage array. Many layers of redundancy, virtualization and failover ensure nearly permanent uptime and unbeatable performance.

Before becoming public, the "cloud" was common place in many banks, big enterprises and corporations where a downtime isn't an option. Advancement in technology meant that this sort of infrastructure became realistic and affordable for most websites. However, the initial cost to setup and support a proper cloud was so high that it effectively priced out of the market many small operators.

Some tried to survive by connecting two old servers and presenting the result as full blown cloud hosting. It's easy to lie to secure a sale, but in the long term, the reality check isn't avoidable. The resulting performance and reliability doesn't live up to the expectations.

It's also essential to keep in mind that the web community started coding and developing even richer websites. In the nineties, people were trying to come with algorithms and tools to compress images in order to spare some bandwidth. At the time, most visitors were "surfing" on modems and similar connections. Now, if the

HD video showed to every visitor takes a few extra seconds to load, the customer would log a support ticket.

People using high speed connections, mobile devices, competition and new technologies make it more and more difficult to properly host a website.

Don't get me wrong. Still to this day, it's possible to install a server with 4 disks on RAID 5 and do some decent hosting with that. But the gold rush is over. Big players have reinforced their position in the market and everything else is a leftover, or a niche.

Myself, I started feeling the heat as my monthly bills were ever increasing. The same websites were using more and more bandwidth and requiring more CPU cycles as their webmasters added features and functionalities.

One of the techniques to survive would have been to do some pruning: terminate all non-profitable accounts and keep the others. I couldn't do that as it went against my values. Sometimes I prefer to fail keeping my values than succeeding by transgressing them. I aim for success but not at any cost. Capping successful customers like the German provider did to me was something to disgusting to contemplate. Charging everyone for the amount of resources used like Amazon Web Services does is a great idea but not viable in my segment of market. Most players were still happily promoting unlimited resources making it difficult for legitimate businesses like mine to survive.

Mother Nature did most of the job for me.

Part 2

My adventure with eBay

I can fill the next 300 pages just by detailing the basics of eBay and including the description of every available option but it's not the purpose of this book. I want you to get added value for every minute you spend with me. If you are not familiar with eBay, you can go to Amazon and get a couple of Kindles about this topic. Here, I am going to share with you my experience, tips and ideas about how to make the best usage of this market place.

There are two approaches in money investment. The classical investor thinks like this: *I have $10'000 and I would to invest on iPhones. I might be open to other smart phones if I find a good deal. I like the idea of selling these technology gadgets. I need to check how is the market doing to see what are my opportunities.*

I have no problem with this approach. It's totally legitimate and sound. But I would like to show you how a tactical investor thinks: *I have $10'000. I need to check how the **market in general** is doing and try to find a hot sector where I can go with the existing flow of opportunities.*

As you see, a tactical investor has no emotional ties with any product in particular. He is a pure opportunist. He can be selling dog food today, antique lace tomorrow and Asian stamps next week. His approach is driven by demand, rather than by offer.

He doesn't come with an offer and searches a market for it. He does just the opposite. He finds a demand then tries to fulfill it. As a small player, it's difficult to create demand for something. Therefore it's better to find an existing demand and consider the product (the offer) less of a problem once the demand is found.

My recommendation is to be flexible, open minded and attack eBay from the tactical point of view. One of the biggest challenges of this method is you have to buy and sells items you've never heard of before. You need to be a quick learner to the point where you can be a matter subject expert in three days in anything. Let me give you an example:

Around 2005-2006, trawling the internet for anything worthwhile, I discovered websites selling masters paintings reproductions. Some of them displayed very large catalogs with dozens of different pieces available to order. China-based artists were reproducing the work or major Western masters like Monet, Renoir, Degas, Pissarro, Sisley and many others. According to them, no printing or transfer techniques were involved. Every piece was carefully hand painted on canvas.

The first thing I realized was that the product wasn't properly displayed and described to give it any value. They weren't even showing the names of the paintings or their original artists. Every piece was given a product number and a table of available sizes. Obviously the supplier was a wholesaler who wasn't overly interested in art or providing a rich end user experience. He wanted to sell quickly and didn't bother with details.

I saw an opportunity here. To be perfectly honest with you, my culture in this particular field was nonexistent. Like many people, I was able to identify La Giaconda from da Vinci and may be a couple of bold colored paintings from van Gogh.

I decided then to spend a week building my culture and learning to talk about it. It was clear on my mind that these items won't sell if they are not presented with their story. When your prospective customer gets the insider view on an object of art, himself can start relating to it and himself would be able to talk to his friends about it. But before inviting friends for the show he needs to buy first.

After just a week spending 10 hours a day online, I started understanding the difference between neo-classicism, impressionism and surrealism. I found myself thrown into a world of colors, stories and passion I didn't suspect before. A few more days later, I unearthed my inner inclinations and discovered that I liked Monet and Dali even if they were so different; the former expressed peace and calm through bucolic sceneries while - for the later - the painting was a projection of his own lovely megalomania.

I went back to the Chinese website and ordered 10 pieces of different paintings I was able to identify, describe in my own words and talk about to a prospective customer. A few days later, TNT delivered a long rounded box. Inside, there was what it looked like a rug for a decent living room. The canvases have been put one on top of each other, separated by plastic sheets then rolled. Judging by the strong chemical smell, they were still wet.

Carefully, I separated them one by one and pinned them in different places. The walls of my tiny apartment were literally covered and the whole place smelled like a workshop.

My initial review revealed that the quality was very different from a piece to another. The main problem was that these artists were unable to reproduce people properly. *The Girl with a Pearl Earring* from Johannes Vermeer looked ten years older, two stones heavier and her expression was totally different than in the original. After this initial review, three canvases went to the rubbish bin. Later, two other joined them because they seemed to have been realized in great haste missing all the details.

The remaining canvases were good enough to be sold. The reproductions of Salvador Dali were the most realistic.

That same day, I started my campaign in eBay, a personal ecommerce website and other smaller auction websites. There have been a maximum of two weeks between the initial idea and going to the market with a finalized product. It was longer than usual. Online economic cycles are shorter. You need to be able to act within hours or days at maximum. If you delay the execution phase you take the risk of arriving too late were the favorable conditions are not there anymore. I had – myself – many projects that I dropped because I couldn't go to the market on time.

On my web hosting business, I used to create products in real time! On day, I had a customer on the chat asking if "we do FTP accounts for backups". I never gave it a thought before but as he was asking, he was creating the demand. I immediately responded: *"We have been working on that product for a while and it's ready for release. We will be publishing the plans and pricing tomorrow morning."* Overnight, I analyzed the market, prepared a web page for the product and by 8 AM the customer was able to order. The tactical approach of the internet marketing is very opportunistic!

My painting business worked very well for a year or so. To avoid lowering the perceived value of my product, I used to put just a few paintings at a time and in limited quantities. Every item was associated with a description, some History and a lot of photos. I even used Photoshop to represent the painting in different interiors and contexts. To make the thing sounds even bolder, every canvas was shipped with a nice "Certificate of Authenticity". I wasn't certifying anything other than the painting was a handmade copy but my customers liked that document. Here, I would like to share two important keys with you:

One: online people buy the product without seeing or touching it as in a brick and mortar store. They buy your description, photos, videos, reviews and whatever material you want to post to represent your product. In fact, you are not selling, you are telling a story. If someone stays in your page for 15 minutes rather than 20 seconds, he is more likely to remember your sale pitch, to bookmark your page, to relate to you and eventually to buy from you. I don't believe in one-line auctions ending with "posted from my iPhone".

Two: when you find a niche, you'll also realize that the market is smaller than what you've hopped for. For example, you can find an item for $10 and sell it for $30. So technically you can turn $100 to $300. But can you turn $100'000 to $300'000? More often than not, it's not possible. Every niche has a weekly volume of market. If people are investing $10'000 a week on a particular niche and you manage to get 5% of that flow then your weekly volume is $500. If you put more products online, the buyers are not going to spend more but your prices – and your profit – are going to fall. For this reason, it's important to be present on more than one niche. If you are well placed on 5 markets and earn $500 a week on each of them, that's already a success for a sole trader activity. To analyze the size of a niche on eBay or Amazon, you can use Terapeak.

I used to sell up to 20 canvases a month with up to %1000 (well one thousand per cent) profit on each. A piece purchased for 20 Euros used to go for around 200 Euros on a no-reserve auction. But you have also to consider my other fees such as import taxes, packaging and also the few pieces I used to discard from each order.

One of the massive flaw with my product – I discovered later – is it's very difficult to make something viable out of a rolled canvas. It needs to be stretched and placed in a support frame before anything else. This operation is difficult and expensive if you want to pay a professional to have it properly done. Don't even think about doing it yourself. It needs special equipment and a lot of experience to give the canvas a uniform tension across its entire surface. As this condition, it will stay perfectly flat in varying conditions of temperature and humidity. This operation is very expensive and skilled professionals are hard to find and usually busy to the point where they refuse to take orders. If I am to do this again, I would ask the Chinese to ship the canvas still stretched on its original frame. It may cost more but it does worth it.

What happened to my niche? The whole thing went to a halt almost overnight. My volume went from 20 canvases a month, to 4, then to 0. In fact as some rules changed with eBay (nothing factual here, I am just assuming), Chinese manufacturers were able to take the market by storm. In a few days, they listed thousands of painting priced at $3 plus shipping fees. They destroyed the market for everyone including themselves. Their texts were written in a mix of Mandarin and poor English. People of arts, are also people of verb so they weren't attracted to these auctions. But in the same time they also deserted my own auctions because the product lost its value.

I had a very good relationship with my provider in China. Sometimes he was even shipping products before receiving payment. By the way, always build this level of confidence with your sources. When you start buying a lot, you will be very well known in the house. They will give you better prices, more flexibility and better terms. All merchants give precedence to repeat customers on anyone else. The manager of the art workshop contacted me and asked why I suddenly stopped buying from them. I explained to him that the market is dead to the point that I was unable to sell a single canvas.

Surprisingly, I also received a letter from a Chinese Custom Officer. He picked up my address in a package and he was trying to see if I was willing to do business with him. I never responded to his letter as his approach sounded dodgy like a hell.

But as you see a niche can dry out overnight. As a sole trader, you have to diversify.

Let me give you another example of another niche where I made money. I identified some demand for gems and stones. I found a website with a rich collection of diamonds and other semi-precious stones. The website was based in Thailand and had some nice reviews from satisfied customers. The name is not relevant (Thaigem.com) because it's closed now. By the way, don't even think about doing business with Thailand. This country is to Asia what Nigeria is to Africa. Risks of fraud, scam and losing money are extremely high.

What I did, is I purchased gems from this online store. Nothing serious to be honest: tiny 0.1 carat diamonds, some topazes, some emeralds and citrines. I paid from 1 to 10 dollars per stone depending on the size and quality of the gem. This price reflected the limited level of confidence I placed on that website. Ideally you want always to make business with partners you totally trust but unfortunately this is not always possible.

I would like to tell you something here: if you want zero risk, you will make zero money. It's as simple as that. Whatever the product you are selling, ultimately your customers are paying you for the risks you are willing to take on their behalf. If you go to the Main Street then visit a good and well established shop to buy something, you take no chance but in the same time you are paying a premium for this peace of mind. Then go and try to sell your newly acquired item: it's too expensive because you got it high in the delivery chain. Your survival online depends on your capacity to take and manage risks. You may lose some money from time to time (like me discarding canvases) but it shouldn't happen too often.

While my first shipment was in transit, I spent a few days learning about gemstones. It's not a rocket science. Just by reading a dozen of Wikipedia articles and taking some notes, I knew enough to sound credible.

At every auction, I explained the story and the meaning of the gem I was selling. I described the color, the cut, the inclusions if any and provided close-up photos downloaded from the provider website. Actually these small things are very hard to photograph! If you don't have a macro lens and a decent camera don't even try.

Did I tell you? It went very well. People liked the stones and they were selling at a steady rate. I found a couple of other providers and often my collection was sold before I received it. Some stones were selling from 10 to 20 times their original price but in a small niche market made of enthusiasts. Sometimes, I received bad batches from Thaigem and had to discard a couple of chipped or broken stones. Apart from very rare incidents, this niche was quietly providing a nice income.

I was running about 10 auctions at the same time maximum. I always waited to sell 3 to 4 stones before placing more in the market. Anytime the prices declined a little, I reduced my number of open auctions until I felt that the people are investing again. Sometimes I noticed a surge of interest for some types of stones and decided to put more of them on sale. I can't know why many people seem suddenly interested to buy the same thing. May be a newspaper claimed that this particular stone heals headache. Or may be a famous pop star said in an interview that it always had this stone in her pocket. You can't know everything but you can perceive how the crowd is moving and you move your open positions accordingly. Basically you need to have the mindset of a short term trader on the stock exchange: you don't want to know why, but how things are moving.

I still remember one particular auction. It was for a 1-inch long artificial emerald. I don't like lab grown gems. They look too perfect and lack this character you find only on the natural ones. I just purchased this one for a couple of dollars and expected to get rid of it for 20 bucks. I started a no-reserve auction with free shipping. I described the emerald explaining that it's not a real gem but it was produced in a lab then cut to its final form. My presentation was full of words like "non-natural" "lab" "artificial" down to the title of the auction. A day or so before the end, the bids sky rocketed to $200! A few hours later it went to $250. I started receiving private message insulting me of selling a piece for green glass for such a price. However, I didn't decide of the price. People were bidding like crazy on a perfectly honest and well-presented description. In the very same time, I had auctions in place for genuine emeralds of various sizes and cuts but no one seemed interested. Again, crowd movements are difficult to predict. My stone went for $350. The highest bidder paid immediately and left a positive feedback on reception. After all, some people are ready to buy a designer bag made in Pakistan for 8000 dollars. Who I am to deny them the right to buy a piece of glass they like for $350? Anyway, it was the first and last time I sold lab created gems. Even if people were ready to buy them, I wasn't ready to sell them.

My gemstones niche came to the halt the same way the painting niche did. A guy from Germany opened an account and offered some gems to sell. That's often the problem online. Whatever you do soon there will be copycats. They have time in hand to analyze your business model but have no creativity at all. They can snoop on your auctions. They read your feedback to see what you are selling for how much but are unable to come with an innovative concept for themselves. For this reason, I recommend to always keep bidders identity private. Therefore when they leave you a feedback, no one can see for what. It will prevent eventual competitors and copycats from reverse engineering your business. Normal customers can still see that positive feedback has been left for you.

The German guy was selling his stones 90% less than my average price on a *"buy it now"* type listings. He had like a dozen of items listed. He was probably selling with a 10% margin and therefore losing money. I sent him a message trying to offer some guidance. Sometimes it's better to help a competitor to make money than seeing him destroying the market for everyone. The guy never responded directly to my message but next day, he had 300 gems listed at dirt low prices. He sold a few stones but the consumer grew wiser and suspicious about the whole thing. A couple of weeks later, some of my auctions went for a dollar or two for stones with much higher value. I wasn't doing well. My competitor wasn't in better position either. The niche was dead. I removed my entire remaining auctions and that was it. To this day, I still have a jar with all unsold gems.

I would like to highlight something here: online, the profit margin is not calculated in percent but in "times". You cannot think like a Wal-Mart: a 10% benefit is actually a loss from the sole trader perspective. I need at least a guarantee to sell my item at least twice its original price in order for me to enter the market. Three times, or 200% benefit is the best if you want something sustainable. As you buy an item for $10 and sell it for $30, you can break it down this way: $10 is your investment back, $10 is your fees/taxes and $10 is your profit.

I give you another example from my experience of a non-sustainable profit. In a store near where I used to live, I found some nice legwear/pantyhose for women. They were selling for 1 Euro a pair and available in many colors and sizes. The quality seemed good for the price. I decided to give them a try. For 3 Euros on eBay plus 1 Euro for shipping, they were immediately a hot seller. Some ladies purchased 5 or 6 pairs at a time. But I was quickly overwhelmed by the burden to process transactions. When a pair sells, I need to go on eBay and check the payment, the size ordered and print the Paypal receipt. Then, I would pick-up an envelope and print a sticker with the shipping address. Inside the envelope, I put my invoice and the ordered item. I double check that the size and the color are correct and I close my envelope. Later that day, I would go to the post office with all my envelopes. Coming home, I would go to eBay and change the status or the order to "shipped".

My profit after tax, Paypal and eBay fees – and the shipping that was at a slight loss – was 1 Euro par order. The process was so cumbersome that I estimated spending 10 minutes in total per order. This included the time to launch the auction, respond to questions, buy the product, package it, print the invoice, print the address label and queue at the post office… Therefore, I could make maximum 6 Euros per hour. I was selling my time at this rate. It didn't worth it.

Don't get me wrong I already sold my time for less than 1 Euro per hour when I needed to put food on the table as matter of urgency. But as my business was getting better, I started giving more value to my time because it is a limited commodity. As I couldn't rationalize my process I decided to stop selling legwear and all low priced items in general.

What to sell on eBay?

It was a time where I was selling for up to 800 Euros a day on eBay. A friend was visiting and he was impressed when he saw the batch of orders I was printing:

- Oh, there is serious money on eBay it seems! I will also open an account and sell stuff

- Yeah, just go ahead and do it, I responded half convinced

- I know what to start with. I have some junk in my attic; I can bring everything out, take photos and put that online

I felt like insulted. I used to spend sleepless nights nervously searching to source a niche that would last six months to a year in the best case. A product, a source and a market: that was my 3-variable equation I used to attack using a brute force method. Every few hundreds products, I used to find one that was somehow worth selling.

To run a successful auction, you need to find desirable items. If you feel that what you have in hand is a sort of "junk" no one would be interested to give you money for it.

Can I buy and re-sell on eBay?

Yes, you can do it. But let me tell you something before. In reality, eBay is not a place where to sell but where to buy. Members are wise and don't buy unless they have the clear feeling that the seller is at loss. As a seller, if you want to get the best value for your products, you have to be very knowledgeable about how the place works. Auction duration, ending time, category, selected options, keywords, country... dramatically influence the exposure and ultimately the final price.

To be fair, there are so many parameters to take in account that many sellers, including professional ones, have sub-optimal listings. The worst listing is 1 line long only with the wrong keywords; it's in the wrong category and has some typos in the title. It means almost no one is going to see the auction until it ends.

Basically I operated with 2 accounts and 2 important tools. I explain everything: I use one account to buy and another one to sell as I don't want to show my customers from where I am getting my products. But literally I am buying from eBay and selling back in eBay. The difference is that my own listings put the product in better light and give it more exposure to its public. As result, it sells for better price.

My most successful strategy was to buy from a country and sell to another. The rationale behind it was the following: if you go to a Wal-Mart downtown Las Vegas, buy a pack of water and try to sell it in the very Wal-Mart parking, you are not going to find any interested customer. Why? Because your source and your selling place are too close to each other. Rather than buying from you in the parking lot, the customer can just walk inside and buy as much water as he wants for better price. Now, take your water from the parking lot and drive 200 miles along the interstate. Find a remote rest area with some vehicles parked there. I claim that your chances to sell your water are one billion times higher in this place than in the Wal-Mart parking lot.

To drive sales, you need to create a *"delta"*, or a gap, between your source and your market. This delta can be just a geographic distance as in the example above, but it can be a linguistic barrier, a minimum purchase order, complicated import laws, a nearly impossible to find source… etc. The bigger is your delta, the bigger is your revenue.

Above I told you that you are paid for a risk you bear in behalf of the customer, here I am adding that you are paid because you can cross a gap a customer can't. When you mix both, you have a powerful concept to sustain your business.

To analyze different markets, I use TeraPeak.com. It's a website that gives extended statics about all eBay – and recently Amazon – market places. You can search for any item or category and see how it is doing in different countries. I used to pay 1 to 2 months of membership every semester just the time for me to analyze various scenarios and see where I am going. Currently I am building my own appliance. It's a tool that automatically analyzes 100'000 products a day in all eBay categories to give a tactical investor point of view. This means it gives the biggest movers and shakers regardless of the category. I am the only person with this tool I expect it to give me an edge over any competition. But it's still in development as I am writing this book.

Other tool I use all the time is AuctionSniper.com. I don't participate to any auction directly. Auction Sniper places my best bid 5 seconds before the end of the auction. It hides my interest in the product until the last moment and let me get it at much better price. If you bid manually, you do it too early and then you start of war of escalation with other bidders. Your profit is not made when you sell your product; it's made when you buy it from your source. The reason is simple to understand: usually the market guides your selling price by placing a cap. But you can influence your own purchase price. The cheaper you get the product, the more profit you make. If you get carried away and pay too much for something – it happens – you cannot increase your selling price because the market won't follow you forever.

Remember this: don't fell in love with any product. If the price goes to high, just pass.

One product line that made me a lot of money was the lingerie. Many people – men and women – spend a lot in lingerie items and they do it online because they get better value for money or are too shy to visit stores. Main Street stores are very expensive also. You can spend a couple of hours checking out and you will quickly realize how many customers are priced out of that market. So here, there is a clear demand and potential to make money.

Lingerie items, except some corsets, are light. It means you can buy lots from everywhere in the world and get them shipped to you for a reasonable price. You also make a lot of scale economy that is not available to people who buy one item at time. Example from one particular provider: cost to ship 1 item from USA to Europe: $53. No one is going to buy a bra for $20 and pay $53 for shipping. But what if we buy 10? The shipping goes to $80. And what's about 20 items? Just $100…

Living in Europe, I think like this: why my customers can't go themselves to the US eBay and buy cheaper from my own sources. Then, I provide my response to every point:

Transport is expensive: I make the transport cheaper buy importing semi-bulk quantities then I pass the economy to my customers. They can get US products but with local shipping rates.

Transport from abroad is slow: I make the transport fast by shipping from the same country.

They don't want to deal with Customs: I deal with them because I am the importer and provide my customers with a hassle free experience.

They don't trust overseas sellers: I take myself the risk and deal with sources in many countries then I provide my customers with a local and risk free service.

They don't speak foreign languages: I do. I even use Google Translate to communicate with some people. But at the end of the day, my customer doesn't have to.

I can even list more bullet points like: advice, discounts, warranty… etc. These represent my added value and the reason (the delta) why my customers buy from me.

Every other day, I used to connect to my provider website and order more items. They typically took one week to ten days to transit. Sometimes the Customs taxed my packages and sometimes they didn't. The post was delivering almost on daily basis. To increase my throughput, I did two things simultaneously. For items that were selling really well, I used to order a lot of them in advance. I was then able to provide same day shipping and next business day delivery when people needed them for a gift or a special occasion. I also listed many items I didn't have in stock. But I announced that there will be some delay for delivery and asked my customers to buy these only if they were comfortable to wait a few extra-days. If I don't have to keep stocks, I can indeed offer better prices.

Every evening, I used to order from my provider all what I sold during the day. I went from a few products in transit when I started, to more than a hundred. A transit product is any item I sold but not delivered to me yet by my provider. What could possibly go wrong?

I remember a week that started as usual but no package to be seen. I was living in France at the time. After a few days without seeing any box, I went to the post office to enquire. Many people were there with similar interrogations. An employee told us – quiet harshly – that strikes were starting in some sorting centers and he can't do anything for us.

I had – at the time – 5 or 6 boxes in transit. I went back home and hoped for the best. By the end of the week, nothing arrived and the newspapers started talking about the strikes gaining momentum.

My inbox was full of emails from impatient customers. A lot of them didn't receive packages I shipped long time ago. Many other paid me but I couldn't do anything as I didn't have the product in hand. Even the money wasn't in my account as I spent it with my own supplier.

My customers were growing impatient. The situation was getting out of hands day after day. Even if it was all over the news that the post office wasn't working, some insisted on getting a refund of items I had dispatched already. Paypal rules are very clear: if you can't provide the proof that you delivered, you refund or the money will be taken from you and the customer paid back. The litigation is automatic: you can't upload a proof of delivery then a refund is issued. Case closed. I profit from this to give you an important recommendation: never ship high priced items without using a tracked or signed for mail. Otherwise, people can claim that they didn't get anything from you and claim their money back. There are too many fraudsters online!

I went again to the post office trying to find a solution. Their employees heard my story with disdain then showed me the door. For them – as they work for the State – a job is for life. They don't care if a small business closes its doors as direct result of their actions. In the TV journalists were talking about horror stories on daily basis. Many companies – who rely on the mail – were thanking their employees and closing.

I tried my luck with my US provider. I sent them an email explaining the whole situation. My offer was simple: I was ready to order again everything that was in transit but I needed a UPS or a FedEx shipment. I was indeed ready to pay for any extra-cost incurred or arrange for the courier to collect on my behalf. With that, I could get my products within a couple of days and try to use local delivery services to dispatch the goods. It would have been at loss anyway, but it was the only option to keep some sort of good standing with my customers.

A few hours later, I received a short email from my US provider: *"We use only USPS. Thank you"*. Packages sent through USPS would invariably go to the French postal system; not a solution.

That same day, I realized that my successful business was over. I started refunding customers until no money was left in the account. My eBay review page was red and full of negative comments. Some people even when refunded, they still feel the urge to ruin your reputation even further.

I declared bankruptcy for that business. The strike lasted for 2 months and caused a disaster for thousands of small and mid-sized companies. Many never recovered. I remember when the postman knocked at the door and delivered my boxes. It was too late and useless. I still sent their orders to a few customers who trusted me and were patient during all this troubled period of time. They even got some extra-items for free. I sold the rest as job lot for a fraction of the original value. Then, the end of the month arrived and had to face another reality: I had no money left to pay the rental of my flats and other bills.

In the morning, I wrote a letter to the landlord and left the place with just a backpack containing my laptop, my documents and what remained in the fridge. When I passed by the mailbox, I dropped the keys inside.

I was leaving the country for good. Until today, I believe that there is no way to make serious business in socially unstable countries like France. Strikes in transports, utility services, administrations, posts… are almost a daily occurrence. This creates a climate when it's impossible to plan, execute and deliver.

Part 3

The Battle of Paris

When I arrived to Lausanne in Switzerland, I found my old aunt waiting with a bread knife at the window. She was cutting her king size mattress in order to get one part for me and one part for her. She was generous that that point and even beyond.

She owned a big freezer full of *"war rations"*. In fact, it contained enough turkey escalopes to survive a 6-month siege. There was also a cupboard in the kitchen with plenty canned tuna.

I spent the next three months painting landscapes in a spare room. I was selling nothing online apart from very occasional hosting services. My network shrunk to a couple of servers and the orders dried out. I went from 5 firm orders a day during my most glorious times to zero in just a few weeks. A troll started publishing fake reviews about my services. He even purchased domain names similar to mine but with different extensions to post insults and threats.

I was too tired to fight back and too broke to hire someone who could do it for me. I stayed at home painting landscapes, eating turkey and sleeping in half a mattress. Days were passing by slowly. I should say "nights were passing by slowly". In reality, I was sleeping most of the day and living by night when I felt more inspired to write or paint.

My new adventure started by an email from my friend Sebastien. He lived in Paris at the time and I had not seen him for a while. The message was turned like this: *"Hi old dude! I created a company with a friend. We do business with television channels and broadcast content online. We need someone with your technical skills. We don't have a lot of money yet but it's coming soon. You have to meet with Stephan. He manages the project and has great ideas about the future. When are you taking the train to Paris? See ya!"*

The same day, I put my ugly paintings to the garbage bin and purchased a one way ticket to Paris. I didn't have the money for a return ticket so failing wasn't an option.

I met with Sebastien in his almost empty two-bedroom apartment in the sixth floor. He lived there with a dog. They were both happy to see me after all that time.

I grasped that life haven't been nice with them. My friend summarized it very effectively:

- A few months ago, I wanted to throw the dog out of the window then jump after

Life is never easy when you decide to fight. He wasn't a sort of guy who goes on benefits and enjoys time at the pub. He wanted to fight or die trying but never give up.

* * *

We went to visit the office. The company rented a couple of floors in an old building south of Paris. The first floor was clean but without any furniture except a table and a couple of desks. The third floor was in an advanced stage of decay. Many windows were broken, electric cables were hanging from the ceiling and the painting was peeling off the walls. I estimated the surface to 300 m2/3200 sqft per floor.

We then met with Stephan. He looked like a smart and soft spoken guy; the sort of person who can sell ice to Siberians in the winter. Even if the bloody building was collapsing around him, he gave the impression to be in control and knowing clearly what to do next to get closer to the goal. He explained that the aim of the company was to provide services for major French TV channels. There were dozens of them and they all had their headquarters in Paris area. He was on first-name basis with many Directors, Producers and Managers in that field.

Basically, he explained, TVs don't create all the content they broadcast. Most often than not, the content is created on order by small media companies. They cover whatever event of interest; they film it, edit it and provide a roll ready to broadcast. That would be our main job. Stephan had also some customers who wanted to have websites online with video content created by the company. They also needed my skills and infrastructure to broadcast some live sport events online.

The money was of a concern but there were negotiations in progress with many investors and prospective customers to seal lucrative deals.

When he finished talking, I found myself dragged into that project. I had no choice anyway. Going to back to Switzerland to paint ugly canvasses and eat oily tuna wasn't an attractive option. The Parisian offer was very vague: now we work our asses off. When the money is here, and there will be loads of it, we share. We shook hands and started.

On my first day at the office, we spent a few hours moving and installing some Apple Mac G3 computers. Don't get me wrong: we had no budget to buy a single item from Apple. They were just old machines that a nearby business gave us for free. It was really kind from them considering that Macs have a very long useful life time. They could have sold them but they preferred to help us starting our project. They also supplied some chairs, a cupboard and a couple of other desks.

I believe in recycling. At every item brought back to life, I felt like a small victory against consumerism. I don't know why someone would decide to throw away a table to go buying another. Both would have a horizontal surface and four vertical legs!

Early evening, the place was clean and the computers ready to start. I launched the operating system installation on each of them and we decided to head home. It was just a 9 AM to 9 PM day. An average day by the crazy standards we were going to set.

My friend Sebastien couldn't afford a car. He was driving a motorbike: a red Honda with a 125 cc engine. It looked impressive but wasn't that powerful. With me as a pillion passenger, it could achieve 100 km/h or 60 mph after a 3-mile uninterrupted acceleration.

It was early November and one of the coldest winters I have ever witnessed over Paris was just starting. Ice patches formed near the Seine River and the metro tube ventilation grids were smoking white and dense. Being a passenger wearing a pair of jeans and a light jacket on a motorbike wasn't an easy task.

Every day, when we arrived home, I had to exercise for half an hour to recover. I felt frozen to the bone sometimes. My knees were still bent and stiff as I walked ridiculously to the bathroom to get some hot water. But still that suffering was part of the fight. If you don't suffer, you are not fighting and if you are not fighting you get nothing. Well, often you can fight and still get nothing. In our particular case, the money wasn't there.

The job was intense and we were all passionate about it. We filmed concerts in the most prestigious halls, operas and theaters of Paris. Our images were broadcasted to millions. But every time a contract was signed, we heard the same story from Stephan: *"Look guys, I have good and bad news here. From the positive side, we are contracted for a show this Christmas. There is 50'000 Euros on the table. At our level, it's Hollywood! A mega-production! No one ever trusted us for project of that size. Now the bad news: the project is going to cost us more or less 48'000*

Euros to realize. I am still working on the figures, but probably we are not going to make a lot of money from it. However, they are giving us this just to see how we deliver. If we work hard, we will be recognized on the market and next project will be the jackpot."

What would you do? We still had the venue to refuse the contract and wait for something else. However, as a new company, we were just eager to build our reputation. Like the guitar man in Elvis song, we were just waiting for someone who says: show'em son, show'em!

* * *

On the D-Day, we rented a couple of trucks and hired almost two dozens of technicians. There were sound engineers, electricians, cameramen, lighting specialists… We also hired a ton of stage Fresnel lighting, cameras, tripods, mixing tables and miles of cables. All this equipment was too expensive to own.

We arrived in the early morning and immediately started deploying. It was an exciting and stressful race against the time. Whatever happened, we had to be ready to record once the show starts at 8 pm.

Everything worked as expected apart from some usual glitches. Only one cameraman called in the last minute to say that his kid was sick and he was with him at the hospital. I took his place and did a respectable job. Probably not as good as him, but it was acceptable.

The concert ended at midnight and we started disconnecting while the public was leaving the place. As every piece fits in a specific dispatch box, it's surprisingly quick to remove and store cinema equipment. In just a couple of hours, everything was boxed and stacked near the loading bays behind the theater. We were waiting just for something: the trucks!

Suddenly Sebastien arrived. He was on foot and dragged me apart:

- We have a problem

- What?

- The trucks are in the parking two blocks from here but we can't get them out as the payment machine is declining my card. If we don't pay, the gate won't open.

- Howe much?

- 40 Euros for both

I gave him my card. I was almost sure that it won't be declined for such amount. I have never seen a Hollywood production stuck because of parking fees.

Our vehicles were released and we left the theatre around 3 AM. We had to drive to our HQ first, unload the equipment to avoid theft then ride the bike to go back home. When we arrived there, Parisians coffees were already open and packed with customers taking their traditional café with hot croissants.

I was frozen and exhausted but I had only a few hours to sleep before attacking again.

* * *

We used six cameras to cover the show. Each of them recorded 3 hours of raw footage. That's 18 hours in total to edit down to a 90 minutes ready to broadcast format. The client wanted us to get rid of some performers. Difficult choice, but it happens all the times. Most concerts are not broadcasted in integrality. TVs keep the duration that fits in their grid.

When the high speed DV cassettes player started uploading the videos, the Mac died. No amount of reboots, hits or knocks fixed it. For that computer, it was the end of the road. We tried with others, but they weren't powerful enough to host the demanding editing software and 18 hours of videos.

I had to step in. The only option was to build a new editing machine. Buying one was out of question as they are too expensive. I found a company card with some credit on it and went shopping for parts. I returned to our HQ with an AMD Phenom processor, a lot of RAM, two massive disks, a motherboard… and a nice big case with quiet fans. An hour later, our new editing station was up and running. My webhosting experience was very handy there. We lost just a few hours on our schedule.

We spent three days in the office working without discontinuation. We just called a neighbor to take care of the dog and make sure he – actually she – doesn't get bored and has enough water and food.

I slept a couple of times inside a heavy curtain that I rolled on the floor under my desk as an improvised sleeping bag. As for Sebastien, I don't know if he ever slept. Anytime I looked, he was focused on his screens and clicking frantically on Avid tools. An ashtray on his desk was rapidly filling-up with cigarettes he was smoking.

We sustained ourselves by eating chocolate, ready soups and pizza leftovers.

It was 5 AM of the fourth day when we eventually decided to leave the office. The job wasn't finished but we launched an export that was going to take six hours to complete. There was nothing for us to do in the meantime.

The streets were empty. We stopped at the only grocer opened at that time. We purchased some biscuits and canned food. Somehow, the owner guessed us:

- *You work for television, don't you?*

For sure: if you are unwashed, smells cigarettes, your eyes are red, you look drained and are buying junk food at dawn, then there is only one profile that fits you: you work for TV. To be fair, you could be a cop also.

I never felt so happy to lie on my bed again. I was shivering from tiredness. After a few-hours sleep and a shower, I was like new. It was Saturday, or even Sunday, neither of us knew really. We decided to go to the office. As long as there was job to do, we had to be there.

It took us a week and a lot of nerves to finish the editing and deliver the order. It was on time for the client to upload it into the broadcast system. They were impressed by the quality of the finished product. The filming, the lighting, the sound, the editing and even opening and closing credits were perfect and up to their specifications.

The total cost for us was 55'000 Euros without counting my 40 Euros for the parking!

As the customer paid only 50'000 Euros, from where did we get the 5000 remaining Euros? You guessed it: from another customer who purchased another project. Stephan was under such a pressure that he sold it at loss also. Here is the Ponzi scheme again! It reminded me my dedicated servers business. We were not making any money. Every new customer was financing the losses accumulated with previous ones. As we were going forward, we needed more and more new comers just to keep up with losses. Even the company credit card was maxed out to 5000 Euros. Then the bank allowed us to go to 8000; then to 10'000.

The market felt that we were desperate and, even if we were doing a great job in terms of quality and delays, no one wanted to give us the fair price. Stephan used to hear the same story again and again:

- *We have a nice project for you. The only problem is that we are low on money this time. I know that 25'000 Euros is not enough for something of that size. But if you do it for us, next quarter we are going to release a new budget and we will give you priority on much better funded contracts. Think also that you are relatively new on the market. I know you and I heard great feedback about you. However, the people I work with don't know you yet. If you do this for us, next time it will be much easier to place you on pole position for a big production...*

The problem is that they kept viciously sending under funded projects toward us. Stephan was considering our work, time and losses as an investment to build our reputation. But it in fact, he was totally wrong. You can still accept lower margins if you are doing your first few customers, but selling at loss is simple madness. A project that actually costs 55k to realize is sold for minimum of 100k in the market. If you want to compromise to enter the market, let's quote for 80k. You are still cheaper than most competitors but selling it at loss is not a winning strategy.

Sebastien and I were working for free and Stephan was living on his saving account and personal credit cards. Every weekday, at noon, he used to go to a nearby restaurant and bring a couple of large pizzas and a big cylinder of coke. It was the only opportunity of having a hot meal. It also gave me this weird feeling that I was working for food.

I remember clearly one day when a customer sent me 50 Euros for a script I fixed for him. I pulled the money and put it on the table at home. With Sebastien, we were looking at it like if it was the proceeds of a bank robbery. What would you do with 50 Euros when you need everything?

We spent a couple of hours deciding how to spend the cash. Predictably, 10 Euros went to a box to buy food for the dog. You can starve, but you can't starve a dog as he depends on you. As we had to commute, we put 20 Euros for the fuel. Spending nights on the carpet at the office somehow reduced our total mileage but still motorbikes don't run on mineral water. With the last 20 Euros we purchased some food and a pack of beer.

* * *

The more projects we were doing, the more miserable we felt. All accounts were deep in red, credit cards were maxed out, the bank was refusing overdrafts and even our suppliers were asking for payment of their old bills before honoring any further order from us.

We did many shows, concerts, DVDs, sport events and published a lot of content online. The audience liked our productions but pizza was still the dearest thing in the office.

Stephan was sad because his wife took the kid and left. Even if he was doing every effort to sleep at home every night, his professional life took its toll from his couple. He was spending hours on the phone with her or writing emails but she quickly decided to fill for divorce.

In the process, they had a house together and elected to sell it and share the money. Paris area is so crowded that once you put a real estate in the market, you get offers well over your asking price within hours literally. The dwelling was advertised and Stephan had the currency in hand in a couple of weeks.

We held a council of war the in third floor between a bunch of electric cables and a stockpile of rotten wooden crates. I was on the opinion to fill bankruptcy for the company and open a new one. The bank would lose its money and the suppliers will be compensated by their business insurance. We had no hard assets to lose apart from some old Macs, worthless furniture and a couple of cameras. Even the building wasn't ours. Our best value was our experience and our address book with many customers ready to order. These cannot be seized by bailiffs. Then we can start over clean and wise.

As for the money, my position was that he buys a house immediately. Certainly smaller than the one he just sold but at least it would be the safest investment possible. A six digit sum may look very sexy to someone eating less than 1000 calories a day but Stephen was a friend before anything else and I wanted him to do the right thing for himself as first priority.

We finished the meeting with no clear conclusion but apparently he wished to use the money to "save" the company. As our business model was fundamentally flawed, I strongly believed that – as is – our project was beyond saving. When things go too far in the wrong direction, it's often better to clear everything and start over rather than trying to apply patches on a sinking ship.

* * *

A few days later a truck was parked in front of the building. His driver and a help were offloading new office furniture. When the desks were installed and chairs put behind, we needed to place people on the chairs. Without consulting us, Stephan started a hiring spree.

Just a week down the line, we had the Director Assistant and the Project Manager. Then came in the Product Manager and another lady with some vague title like Communication Assistant or something that sounded similar… They were all on permanent contracts with more than decent salaries. They showed from 9 to 5 and started their day by a team meeting. The rest of the time, they wrote emails, prepared Power Point presentations or played FreeCell.

Contractors, painters and electricians arrived and started a huge building site in the third floor. The goal was to repair and rehabilitate this devastated area and setup a recording studio.

It seemed like the situation was getting out of hands. Stephen was spending like no tomorrow. Once he smelled the money, our associate and nonetheless friend was no longer the same. I tried to approach him carefully and highlight the problem. But he had always the same pitch:

- *Look, if you want to play big, you have to look big. To attract money, you have to show that you have money! Soon, I am going to invite investors to visit our building and discover what we do. If they see that we are a working company with many employees and nice office space, they are going to help us. If we look ugly, they won't be interested.*

I saw where he was coming from. But if we wanted to fake it, it would have been less expensive to hire actors and escorts for a day or two. With 100'000 Euros cash in hand, you can't reasonably hire 5 people on 50k/year each especially when the company is not making profits.

In a business, many expenses can be increased or decreased very quickly giving flexibility in managing a difficult cash flow. However, hiring employees in permanent contracts gives strict and non-negotiable obligations. In Europe, it's not possible to hire and dismiss people at will. Employees enjoy a lot of legal protections. In France you can't lay off someone unless you satisfy a very complex set of legal and procedural requirement; and even though you must compensate the person you let go. Literally you give her worth of 3 to 12 months of salary, depending on her seniority, for her to go peacefully. These laws were introduced to protect employment but in fact they do exactly the opposite. Many companies would need more people but managers are too afraid to hire because it could be a one way ticket to disaster.

Anyway, the investors came in. They ate cake, drink Champagne and exchanged business cards; and that was it. The only things they gave were kind words promising to "follow our activity with big interest" and "meet in a year or two to see if we can find synergies".

Sebastien and I were sad and disappointed. We worked days and nights for ten months without taking holidays or days off. We moved mountains but were still working for food while new hires were receiving more money than we could've ever dreamt of. But that what happens when you work for free. People never realize your value and even if one day they have money, they prefer to pay anyone else but not you. Because you are free.

If one day you are to enter in a venture with your work only, bill your hours as an investment. For example, I could have said that my average price is $50 per hour. Then, I keep a monthly log of hours done. If I bill 200 hours a month, that means I am investing $10'000/month on the venture. After 10 months, my share value in the partnership is $100'000. It's actually giving work for shares. As an investor, I would have been in stronger position to vote and even veto decisions which are against my best interests. In the worst case scenario, I would have cashed my shares and left with some money.

If you have to keep only one major lesson from this book it would be to never work for free. As professional, even if you want to offer a free service because you have strategic reasons to do so, bill your customer and put 100% reduction. It looks much better to give a $5000 invoice with an exceptional 100% discount than saying: "it's free" which would be always understood as: "it has no value whatsoever".

I felt treated as a worthless person in that partnership and I had only myself to blame for it.

With Sebastien, we started changing our pattern to get a proper life. We no longer wanted to do the night or work weekends I declined my participation to a project because it would have involved too much work for a pizza a day. There were also other major flaws in that particular project but I was no longer keen to give advice for free. Later, that project bit the sand.

I started walking in Paris; going where Japanese tourists crowd to take photos. Soon Eiffel Tower, les Champs Elysees and the borders of the Seine had no secrets for me. I chatted with tourists, got involved in online communities and slept for ten hours in a row. Sebastien also changed his life style. He was going to the office every other day and staying only for a short period of time.

* * *

The Director Assistant was the first person to give a strong signal that something was seriously wrong. She went on holidays for a week and never came back. She didn't even bother to send a resignation letter to save the form. Stephen left her some voicemails but she never returned his calls. That was worrying because from her position, she had access to all the financial details.

Stephen was holding to the same communication line but it sounded less and less realistic:

- We are doing well. I am negotiating big projects. I have a customer in Hong-Kong who needs a partner to make some short films in France. I am in talks with all the TV channels for which we did work at loss and now some of them are ready to honor their promise and give us projects with better funding... We may get a mega contract to cover sports for a whole season...

At the end of that same month, the company was closed forever.

Things happened too quickly. It was payday and the bank called to inform that salaries couldn't be paid. The account was in red.

You can always negotiate with suppliers to get some delay to pay your bills. If you are in difficulty, most of them would agree to allow you a few days to a few weeks to settle. Some would even write-off a bill in exchange of renewing a service contract or giving them some exclusivity. Even the most heartless banker would give you more time to clear an overdraft or would remove incurred fees. However, the day you can't pay salaries, you are dead. You are not entitled to negotiate anything with employees. Either you pay or the matter goes immediately to the nearest Court. In only 4 months, Stephen spent all the money from the sale of his house. That money, rather than helping us to succeed precipitated our failure.

I was sitting on my desk trying to fix a script we used to convert videos in order to publish them online. These scripts are too painful to maintain because codecs keep changing all the time. Suddenly, a man showed at the door: old, gray hair, gold frame glasses, massive brief case and impressive shoes size. He looked very serious; official.

Stephen greeted him solemnly like if he was the angel of death then both marched to an office. Half an hour later, the man left and carefully closed the door behind him.

I immediately went to see Stephen. He looked ten years older. He was served with official documents that were scattered across his desk. They bore stamps is red ink and scribbled hand signatures. There were numbers; numbers everywhere. Banks, salaries, taxes, suppliers, interests, arrears, fines… the company owed money to half of Paris. The master piece of the whole lot was the final document from the Court: you cease business upon reception.

I think I never turned a page of my life so quickly. I didn't ask any question. I didn't log out from my computer. From Stephen's office I walked directly to the street. I took the bus to the train station and from there a TGV to Lausanne, Switzerland. My half mattress was still waiting for me.

The Battle of Britain

This time, I wanted to fight back. I had to change my methods and attack the problem from a totally different perspective. My aunt was fully supportive and told me that all what I did wasn't to earn money, but it was a school of life. All what I did was to get to know myself, push my limits and be aware about my value.

If you don't know your value, you are like a lotto player oblivious that he has a winning ticket in his pocket. He will never cash it and loses millions without ever realizing it. This happens all the time.

From all the people you meet in your life, few will positively help you to find yourself. Many will just take advantage of what you are because they are good at taking from others. But don't expect any gratitude or recognition from them.

If you don't recognize yourself, nobody would do it for you. That's one of the most valuable lessons I learnt from these five years pissing against the wind.

I started thinking about my professional experience and writing a resume. Without lying, I had to glorify my past activity. My struggle in Paris became "Special Technical Consultant". Nobody needs to know that I did it for food. My webhosting experience became "IT Services Provider". Selling paintings from China was placed under the label "International Art Consultant". I couldn't find any family friendly description for my lingerie business, so I decided to skip it.

After a few days, I had a nice CV with two major issues. It was too long. A CV is not a book or a life story. In many places, everything must fit within one or two pages. In reality, most hiring managers I spoke with don't care about the length. They even prefer to know more rather than less. But still, it's important to stick to the rules to pass most filters.

My second issue was that my experience looked illogical and inconsistent. Many items were overlapping or conflicting. How can you explain that you spend the night fixing servers in a data center then selling cheap acreage in Arizona during the day? Most people would find my CV funny or original but it wouldn't fit with the straight and predictable profiles they look for.

Watching the news, a couple of journalists were interviewing a renowned career specialist from Canada. I noted her name and dropped her an email asking what to do about inconsistencies on my resume. At my surprise – and as busy as she was - she responded within a few hours. She explained that the CV is a document that should focus on a service or a set of skills I am selling. In that sense, it was advisable to avoid any experience that has the potential to distract from that goal. According to her, if had various skills that appeal to different markets, I was entitled to write different CVs. Each of them would put the highlight of one aspect of my professional life.

Following her advice, I wrote a resume with only my computing-related experience. It looked much shorter and cleaner. Then, I went to eBay and purchased a CV rewriting service provided by a lady with "30 year experience". She did a great job by cleaning my draft and editing it to something that sounded professional. I also created a LinkedIn profile matching that CV.

It was almost midnight when I got everything polished and sent my first batch of emails. Don't worry, I didn't send millions of them. Just three but personalized and targeted. I selected these companies in Britain because it's the only place in Europe where people are open to baroque profiles. In Switzerland if you want to make hamburgers with onions, you must show a diploma indicating that you can indeed make hamburgers with onions. I am slightly exaggerating here, but you got the idea. In France, universities belong to the State and they are almost free. Many young people spend up to ten years in that system. As result, any available place of work causes an outrageous escalation between candidates to who spent most time in the university. The branch of studies is not relevant as the time done.

The British market is very similar to the US one. Hiring managers are very pragmatic. They don't rate people on their capacity to pass exams, but to do the job. The knowledge itself is assessed by technical interviews which are performed regardless of the presumptive or claimed capacity of the candidate. Therefore, everyone has a genuine chance to demonstrate his abilities. This is also an Eldorado for self-learners which are summarily dismissed in countries such as France or Switzerland.

I sent my emails with resume and cover letter then went to bed. When I got up, I found two responses back from recruiters keen to have a chat with me. Almost 70% of conversion rate! That was the power of targeting rather than spamming blindly. I called both of them. I was nervous because I felt a new page turning in my life.

Both interviews went well. They asked me generic questions about my skills, motivations and my relocations plans to Britain.

Later that day, I received a call from a hiring manager for a data storage company. He said that he was "impressed" by my CV and he spent most of the time trying to sell the position to me. To induce some nervosity, I disclosed that I was interviewing elsewhere also.

At end of the conversation, he asked me I can fly to Britain as soon as possible for a face to face interview. It was Thursday afternoon; too late to make something happens on Friday. We agreed for Monday first thing in the morning.

I spent the rest of the day arranging my flight and finding a temporary accommodation. A cheap hotel in Reading, Berkshire, charged me 200 Pounds for a week. It wasn't too bad for a deal but it puts me in a situation where I couldn't buy a return flight from Easyjet. As many times in my life, I had to buy a single ticket for my destination. Failure wasn't an option.

I landed in London Stansted and found my way to Reading. It was my first time in the country and everything seemed to work the opposite way as in the Continent.

I spent the weekend consulting documents and preparing for the interview. By Sunday evening, I knew everything about the company: their History, their products, their major customers, their partners, number of employees, capitalization, shares movements… While I wouldn't quality this knowledge as essential, often it can make a difference between you and a candidate who performed the same way. There would be always an occasion when this search plays in your favor.

On Monday morning, I wore my suit. I couldn't recognize myself in the mirror; I looked so smart. I had to exercise a little to feel comfortable in that outfit. Feeling like on disguise, I left my room to be on time for the appointment.

It was quiet a walk but certainly shorter than from Schiphol airport to the data center. And I wasn't pulling a trolley full of servers, wasn't I?

* * *

I was greeted by the hiring manager: John; a nice guy. Not that tall be heavy like many people in the industry. He asked to me follow him to a meeting room and offered a seat. I needed one for what he was going to announce:

- We tried to call you during the weekend

At the time, I owned a gray and bulky handset Nokia 3210 with a pay as you go SIM. I had almost no credit in there so activating the roaming wasn't an option. He then went on to explain:

- Well, we had an "all hands" meeting on Friday. It was late because everything is managed from California. Well, they told us to freeze recruitment until further notice. I don't how long it is going to last. May be a few weeks, may be a few months but as result, the position doesn't exist anymore. I am sorry.

Big John was really embarrassed but there was nothing he could do. As an apology, he offered me to go through the technical interview as a training opportunity. I accepted the offer. It was better than nothing.

John left and a technician came in. He introduced himself an asked me about my experience with Linux and Windows. We started a chat. It was an open and equal-to-equal discussion. The situation being what it was, he didn't want to ask silly questions or bring in any pressure. He was impressed by my data center experience and the number of issues I solved alone. A profile like mine "would have been an asset to their team but unfortunately"... you know.

I found myself on the street with a light rain pouring over me. My bad luck hit again. It was hard to imagine any form of prosperity starting from that ugly situation: being abroad, out of money and out of prospects. One thing kept me alive: I wasn't out of ideas.

Back to my hotel room, I picked up my old laptop and went searching for any place with free public Wi-Fi. I found that pictogram on a McDonald's restaurant door. I went in there, purchased a basic hamburger and sat in a corner. I had to find a job; now!

My CV was ready and I had in my favorites a list of jobs search engines. Even if I was in panic-mode, I had to be very selective and target only positions that suited my profile. My filter was a little bit relaxed than usual, but I had to keep misses a low as possible. It was matter of survival. I couldn't afford to spend money on transportation and waste my time going after jobs that were not for me.

I was writing another motivation letter when a McDonald's employee came in and asked me to disconnect my computer from the power outlet immediately. As my laptop was old, the battery couldn't hold more than 5 to 10 min worth of charge. Keeping it plugged was a matter of life or death. However, I had to disconnect and within minutes, my PC stopped working. You know, I really love Britain, God Save the Queen, and all this, but there is something I would like to kindly rant about. Neither in France, Switzerland, Germany, United State, Africa, Asia or any other place I lived in, visited or know about would a fast food employee do the "extra-mile" and ask someone obviously seeking a job to unplug his PC from the corporate power grid. While I met with many great people in Britain, it's still the country where I found the most small, self-important and arrogant individuals. You'll find many of them working in the parking enforcement industry or receptionists at a General Practitioner surgery.

Later, I went to a pub and sat at small table in a corner. There was a plug and nobody cared that I pugged in laptop in there. Employees and patrons were watching football and applauding loudly.

I also contacted an old customer of mine. I knew he was interested in buying some hardware for his company. In Switzerland, I had a couple of decent servers taking dust under a bed. He bargained them down to 800 Pounds. A fraction of their actual value but I needed cash immediately. Once we agreed on the deal, he sent a Western Union and I asked my aunt to open the door for him when he comes in to collect. That expedient bought me some time but I had to find a job or go back to Lausanne and paint canvases in the night.

That same week, I secured 3 interviews. The market was very dynamic and many IT companies were hiring. For once, I find myself in the right place, at the right time. Usually in my life, I was always either too soon, or too late and missed the train. It's because I kept trying that I had a hit.

The first interview didn't go well. They forgot about the appointment and no one was ready to meet with me. I spent half an hour waiting in the lobby until an old manager came in. He was unfriendly like a hell. He just asked a couple of questions in hurry then left. One day lost.

Another agency booked me for an interview but this one didn't go well also. Apparently the agency tried too hard to push my CV for a Java Programmer position. I don't code Java and never claimed so. However as they make their money by providing candidates, some agencies are unprofessional and chance any profile to any position hoping to get a fit. It's a sort of fulfillment by brute force.

On the first question, I realized that I was in the wrong place. I felt embarrassed and worse than this, I started to lose my confidence. The initial success that justified my presence in Britain seemed like a faint stroke of luck. Since landing in the country, nothing worked as expected.

My third interview was with a company that does cryptography and secures networks of banks and big corporates. I worked hard from the pub to prepare the interview as the position looked very interesting.

Usual wait in the lobby; secretaries peeking; hurry people passing: the solitude of the candidate lingering before an interview.

I was approached by a young bloke; firm handshake. He then asked me to follow him. Three guys were waiting in a small office. Two of them asked questions and the third was observing while messaging intermittently with his mobile. I felt all the time in control and marking points. After half an hour, I was on the street again.

The phone rang, it was the recruiter: I was hired.

Conclusion

The salary was a low ball: 24000 Pounds (38000 USD) a year. But I accepted it as way to pay my entry ticket and put a foot in the ladder.

Just a month later, John left me a voicemail. His company was hiring again and he was keen to offer me the job I came in for. As I passed all interviews already, I had just to sign and go. The same day, I met with him after my shift. He was alone in the office. He stayed late just to meet with me. He offered 37000 Pounds (60000 USD).

My aunt was right: all what I did online during the last five years was just a school. I was learning the job; the hard way.

It was difficult for me to quit my first employer after such a short period of time, but the money on the table made is a non brainer.

Father John was a control freak. Even if I used to fix half the worldwide company cases, he was always monitoring my activity and interfering any time he saw me checking my personal emails or reading the latest news. One day, he even asked me to start taking fewer cases because I was causing some embarrassment to the rest of the team.

The company had one team in USA and another one in Britain to treat about 300 support requests a month. I used to fix 150 of them single-handedly and still find room to read my emails or read the news.

When I was working in my room 16 hours a day, I had no time to waste. I developed a methodology to address issues effectively and lower back and forth interactions with the customer. It wasn't in my best interest to play for time and drag things for a while. I was covering alone and using different names for simulate a team. In the IT industry, they are far from this culture. They all claim that they are "busy" but in fact, they run with bloated teams, inefficient methodology and irrational processes.

In Switzerland, there is a popular proverb that says: *"doing and undoing is not working"*. In corporate environments, I found people actually working for 30 minutes then struggling with the disorganization for the rest of the day.

What shocked me is the fact that teams made of smart people don't necessarily combine their intelligence, but often their imbecility. The worst of each person is added to the pool to create a group with a resulting IQ comparable to a small monkey.

The internal bureaucracy takes also its toll. Something that could be done in five minutes, takes 3 days because too many people, departments, managers, administrators... are involved without brining any added value apart from their presence.

Last but not the least: politics cause disasters. I don't know for other fields of the economy, but I can certify that IT companies are rotten by politics, personal agendas, groups of interests and many other vectors that don't have anything to do in a professional environment.

The net result is that many companies pay 10'000 of man hours for every 1000 hours of actual work they need. The rest is just wasted human time and resources. I will develop that in another book dedicated to these problems.

I spent almost a year with John. Retrospectively, he wasn't a bad guy but he was stuck in a system where nor himself or anybody else could perform well. The company was losing money and every quarter was even worse than the previous one. During my time there, at a couple of occasions, they laid off some employees. The morale was low and people were always gossiping at the coffee machine or in the bathroom. The million dollar question was: who is next?

When I received a cold call from a recruiter, I didn't have to think twice. His client was looking for an experienced Storage Engineer with some European languages. They found me on LinkedIn and were keen to talk at my earliest convenience.

I had just one phone interview and a quick face to face and they were ready to sign. They offered 47000 Pounds (75000 dollars) salary. They also threw in a health insurance, stock options and training opportunities in California. I couldn't believe that just a year earlier I was working 100 hours a week for a daily slice of pizza.

Big John almost fainted when he received my resignation letter. But I still had to endure one month working my notice period for him.

My new job was technically challenging but more exciting because I was working with production systems of big names: banks, telecommunication companies, government agencies... I was no longer troubleshooting webhosting servers from my room, but multimillion dollar systems which were at the core of major corporations.

I spent almost 4 years in this position. At the end, I was one of the longest serving guys in the team. My job was appreciated and they gave me a promotion that involved more responsibilities but they didn't follow with more money. My salary increased to 50000 Pounds ($80000) a year only.

One day, I was helping a new hire in a position lower than mine. I remember that he didn't perform very well at the interview but the company was desperate as our customer base grew significantly while a couple of strong engineers left us for a competitor. At the time, we had an option to work some yearly holidays for the company in exchange of more money in the paycheck. He was playing with that option and he told me that selling days wasn't worth it because when he renounced to X days, he got only Y Pounds more after tax.

I remembered the values he gave and did some math. With the figures he freely elected to disclose, he gave away his salary! The dude was flying at 55000 Pounds a year. This is how some corporates value their longest serving talents!

Without giving any specific information, I challenged my manager about my own salary. He told me that new contracts had to be aligned for current market while old contracts don't have to be.

Well, I had another venue to align my salary against the market: to put my resignation on the table and let them struggle with their customers and a bunch of new hires.

At that time, I used to receive emails from 2 to 3 headhunters per week. I decided to call one of them and he invited me for a drink in London. He had one nice position that would be ideal for me: creating and managing a new support department for a US company attacking EMEA market. They were ready to put 70'000 Pounds ($110'000), plus bonus, plus health insurance, plus stock options... I was sold before he finished. After a serious round of interviews, they were 6 of them in total, I signed a contract.

* * *

Today, I am a respected professional with a strong CV, skills and experience. Many doors are opened to me as recruiters are chasing almost on daily basis. I learnt a lot during the recent years, but most important lessons I ever had, were during these long, dark and lonely nights running my business from my room. I believe that you can go as far as you want when you have the basics right. People, corporates or organizations always fail for basic and simple things. You will never find a complex scenario to justify a failure.

My webhosting company still exists but it shrunk to one single server. I don't make any money from it but I keep it for my experimentations, giving away hosting to my friends and also remembering the old good time. This machine doesn't belong to me. I prefer to rent it and have the data center fix it when it fails. It doesn't fail that often: I schedule only one reboot a year. If I had such a machine years ago, I would have made serious money.

I have a driving license and a car I purchased with zero miles in the odometer. I no longer have to carry heavy loads, move house by bus or suffer unnecessary hardship. I am blessed that I didn't hurt my health too badly during all those crazy years.

Now paying my rent is no longer an existential question. I have money in my bank account and a couple of credit cards to pay for my holidays trips, help my family or go to the restaurant.

My friend Sebastien left Paris a few years ago. He is now living with his wife in a small French village. We are still close and he was my witness at my wedding this year. He never talked to Stephan again and doesn't want to hear about him anymore. He held him responsible of the failure of our project and many issues that happened after that.

The day I left Paris, Stephan closed the business in compliance with the court order. All his professional and personal accounts were deep in red and the bank froze them. He couldn't pay for his rental and ended-up evicted from his apartment. A cameraman we used to hire gave him a bed literally saving him from the street. It took him more than a year to recover, find a job and move to place of his own. I am still in contact with him. We exchange a couple of emails or phone calls a year. He is no longer looking to open a business.

My friend who brought me into the spamming business also left Paris. Too many people were looking for him for money and ventures that didn't work as planned. He is hiding somewhere in the world. Last week, he contacted me to ask for a favor. He wanted the list of all possible combinations of the Euro Million lottery. Apparently he was trying to convince an investor to play them all. I stayed after hours at my job, wrote a script and used one of our most powerful machines to compile the list of him. I told him that if this venture fails, the world would be too small to hide. Even if you play all lottery numbers, you have no guarantee to get all your money back. In fact, for that draw you may have to share your winning lot with many other players who played just a few bucks but were lucky to hit the jackpot.

My aunt passed away a couple of years ago; a cardiac arrest. I wouldn't have made it without her constant presence, counseling and assistance. She at least died knowing that I am successful and that she didn't have to worry about me anymore. I am sometimes nervous because that half mattress doesn't exist. Now I feel like a trapezist jumping without any safety net. I don't have the right to fail.

I won't fail. But if needed, I can still start a life with a backpack, 50 Euros and a one way ticket.